buddhism *for* mothers

Mother of two small children, Sarah Napthali is a practising Buddhist, who has pillaged wisdom from the main Buddhist traditions. Former world traveller, former human rights activist, former corporate trainer, interpreter and technical writer, she now raises her two sons and hopes to eventually return to her business in writing services.

buddhism *for* mothers

A calm approach to caring for
yourself and your children

sarah napthali

ALLEN&UNWIN

First published in 2003

Allen & Unwin
83 Alexander Street
Crows Nest NSW 2065
Australia
Phone: (61 2) 8425 0100
Fax: (61 2) 9906 2218
Email: info@allenandunwin.com
Web: www.allenandunwin.com

National Library of Australia
Cataloguing-in-Publication entry:

Napthali, Sarah, 1967– .
Buddhism for mothers: a calm approach to caring
for yourself and your children.

Bibliography.
Includes index.
ISBN 1 74114 010 2.

1. Mother and child. 2. Parenting. 3. Dharma (Buddhism).
I. Title.

649.1

Internal design by Sandra Nobes
Set in 11/14 pt Adobe Garamond by Midland Typesetters, Maryborough, Victoria
Printed by Griffin Press, South Australia

10 9 8 7 6 5 4 3

contents

acknowledgments

MELANIE LOTFALI, COLLEEN SATTLER AND JOANNE FEDLER are friends who have offered spiritual support and masses of sympathetic joy. Between them, they have reviewed chapters, made eloquent contributions and helped me on my own spiritual path. Susan Murphy has generously allowed me to quote from her exquisite writings and Anne Cushman has generously provided her entertaining article 'Mothering as Meditation Practice'. Other inspiring contributors have been Betsy Coombs and Chittaprabha from the Western Buddhist Order, and Zen teacher Subhana Barzaghi. I thank the many mothers who have allowed me to include intimate details of their lives. Some prefer not to be named and I appreciate them trusting me to protect their privacy.

I thank my husband, Marek, who despite a lack of interest in all things spiritual has been supportive of and helpful during my writing of this book, and my sons Zac and Alex for allowing me to drag them around libraries and for being outstanding spiritual teachers. My mother-in-law Barbara flew out from Poland to literally hold the baby while I finished draft two. I thank her and take inspiration from her strong desire to be helpful. Thank you to my father Bryan Napthali for all the times he minded the boys, and to my mother Sue, my friend Viv and my sisters Amanda and Jane.

A final thank you to the editors Colette Vella and Jane Gleeson-White for their efforts and insights as well as to Annette Barlow and Emily O'Connell for all their encouragement.

preface

AT THE AGE OF 24 I was living in Jakarta, Indonesia, teaching English. In 1991 Jakarta was an uncomfortable city where you spent hours sitting in traffic breathing air thick with pollution. Frustrations abounded: phones never worked, the immense noise level of 10 million people seldom dropped and as a foreigner you constantly dodged hawkers, beggars, taxi drivers and the curious. Open sewerage canals lined the streets. At first I loved the way this city contrasted with home—its ceaseless buzz, the sensory feast—but eventually, as is the pattern, culture shock set in and I handled it gracelessly.

Although Indonesia is predominantly Moslem, I chanced on a book by an Englishman, Guy Claxton, called *The Heart of Buddhism—Practical Wisdom for an Agitated World*. Never had I read such radical material and I started highlighting the most inspiring points. My highlighter soon ran out. I urged friends to read the book so I could explore the issues with others—and over the years I have kept returning to it.

The teaching that first struck me with its potential to stir up my life was that humans tend to live in a state of complete delusion. We assume that the way we see the world, the people in it and ourselves, is the way it is. Buddhism teaches that our perceptions are way off the mark and lead us to waste energy striving for an illusory happiness. I could immediately apply this to my bout of culture shock: I could take a fresh look at the irritations around me, see them in new ways and respond differently. Daily annoyances suddenly had the potential to teach me.

Buddhism encourages us to become aware of all our perceptions, thoughts and beliefs, to overcome the misconceptions that ensure our suffering. Learning to be aware of the workings of our minds we find the power to transform our experience of life. In the words of the Buddha:

> We are what we think. All that we are arises with our thoughts.
> With our thoughts we make the world.

According to Buddhist teachings, our capacity for happiness depends on the state of our minds. And as there is no God-figure in Buddhism, responsibility for managing our minds and reshaping our worlds lies completely in our own hands.

For years *The Heart of Buddhism* constituted my whole understanding of Buddhism until eventually I started to read more widely. I dabbled in Buddhist meditation techniques but was more enchanted by Buddhism as a philosophy than as a practice. I certainly benefited from using Buddhism as a philosophy—the only problem was that it was never supposed to be a philosophy. Rather than being an additional compartment of our lives, true Buddhism is something you practise every moment you can remember to.

In my twenties I could never quite believe that closing my eyes and concentrating on the rise and fall of my breath could be a productive use of my time. I wanted to get things done, to meet people, develop my brain, improve my skills—and have plenty of fun. Although these pursuits were often enjoyable, eventually I lost contact with most of the people I'd met and forgot most of what I'd learned. With hindsight I now realise I would have benefited more from concentrating on spiritual development, for I would now be further along a spiritual path.

When I came to live a drastically different lifestyle in my child-rearing thirties, Buddhism became even more relevant. I wanted to be a wise mother, yet often caught myself thinking and behaving in ways I wasn't proud of. I felt the need, especially for my children's sake, to become a more virtuous person: more patient, more compassionate and more positive in outlook. I knew this couldn't happen through mere wishing—it would take commitment and discipline.

So I started to take spiritual development more seriously. As a mother of one running a business from home, this was challenging and I have to admit to the odd month where I failed to give matters spiritual any attention at all. At other times I found opportunities to meditate daily. Still, I longed to go away on silent retreats for intensive periods of meditation. As a new mother such chunks of time weren't available, but I could still see that combining the spiritual and the day-to-day was powerful. My irregular meditation practice did make me calmer and more positive. Applying Buddhist teachings did freshen my outlook and make my life run more smoothly.

When I was pregnant with my second son I was aware of the challenges ahead and more than a little anxious. I knew that along with the jubilation, relief and 'hormonal high' would come the sleep deprivation, the long hours at home and the difficulty of finding time for myself. I wanted to be mentally prepared, to prevent any slide into depression. Again I escalated my commitment to Buddhist practice: meditating regularly, attending courses and trying to live more mindfully, compassionately and ethically.

I wrote the first draft of this book during that pregnancy, but once the second baby arrived I became more aware of just how difficult parenting could be. I added a chapter on anger—with the challenges of juggling two, I was gobsmacked at how my fuse had shortened when dealing with my first son Zac who was three and a half. I had never experienced much anger with Zac before baby Alex came along. Intense frustration, irritation and despair, yes! But never this violent anger where I wanted to swear and physically lash out. Although I never hit Zac I did sink a fingernail into his thigh once and suddenly I saw that acts of violence against children weren't necessarily committed by monsters but by parents like me. Alarmed, I knew that anger would become quite a theme for my spiritual practice. But I was not alone. Many of the mothers I spoke with were meeting and wrestling with the same beasts. In Buddhism, anger is seen as unhelpful and harmful and the teachings constantly emphasise the importance of freeing ourselves from its grip.

Being thrust into parenthood can provoke inner turmoil for a mother yet parenting literature invariably focusses on nurturing children rather than the mothers who struggle to raise them. Books about the inner lives of mothers tend to be depressing reports portraying us as victims suffering a lifestyle that nobody warned us about. I felt the need for a book that acknowledged the sorrows, as well as the joys. A book that offered coping strategies that not only worked but could renew our lives on a deep level.

Popular Buddhist literature also pays scant attention to the specific situation of mothers. It assumes you have time for daily meditation sessions, active involvement in a spiritual community and lengthy retreats. Examples of Buddhists are too often celibates, nuns, monks, world travellers, celebrities—people who can teach us a lot but who aren't facing the everyday challenges of parenting.

Buddhism for Mothers is not a parenting manual but a book for mothers. By presenting some Buddhist practices, it provides a way for mothers to reconnect with their inner selves and become calmer and happier. I have asked scores of Buddhist mothers, 'How does practising Buddhism help you as a mother?' The most common answer I hear is the same four words, 'It makes me calmer.' And with calmer, happier mothers, our families can only benefit.

In this book I want to use mothers' lives as the starting point: what are the issues of concern to mothers and how can Buddhist teachings help? Some of the themes I explore include the benefits to us and our children of living in the moment, how we can feel calm, and how we can manage our anger and worries. I also discuss the effects of motherhood on our relationships with our partners, friends and relatives, as well as with our own selves.

In Appendices 2 and 3, I recommend helpful books and websites suited to the interests of mothers.

I should say from the outset that I have taken an eclectic approach to Buddhism in this book, drawing on gems from across the main Buddhist traditions. At times I've felt like a thief pillaging Buddhism for treasures of use to mothers and agonised over whether my approach was in tune with the spirit of Buddhism, which encourages us not to mix and match the teachings but to settle with one tradition, headed by a qualified teacher. Of course there is immense overlap between the traditions, and the heart of Buddhism—the core teachings—is the same across the traditions. Still, in some instances I might have made the odd sweeping statement that doesn't sit perfectly with all schools. My eclectic approach also means that this book is only a starting point, a taste of what Buddhism has to offer. Any serious practice of Buddhism needs to be within one tradition with one qualified teacher and it's up to each individual to choose where in the vast world of Buddhism they slot in—if at all.

I must also add that I am a very ordinary woman. Most Buddhist writers have a list of credentials as long as any reclining Buddha. Some of them could be enlightened. Most have spent years in retreat and have had some very impressive teachers. I, on the other hand, have never been on a retreat of more than two nights (and I had to take my sons) and can't remember ever meditating for more than an hour and a half. I'm no spiritual giant but rather someone who is bumbling along, constantly humbled by how much I still need to progress, but also amazed at how much Buddhist practice can improve my day.

It's my hope that through being so ordinary, I can help mothers leading 'normal' lives with all the usual constraints, to understand some of the treasures Buddhism has to offer. That said, I urge readers to keep investigating long after finishing this book. In particular, return to the source and look into the translations of the Buddha's words in the popular Dhammapada and other scriptures.

Still, in the final analysis it matters little what I, or anyone else, have written, or even what you find in the scriptures, for the simple reason that it is your own experience that fuels your learning. The lessons that your own life is teaching you are the most reliable and the most useful. It's your journey. Buddhist teachings provide an excellent explanation of whatever is going on along your way, as well as presenting a well-travelled path to happiness.

CHAPTER 1

buddhism *and* motherhood

MOTHERS OF SMALL CHILDREN are on their own. Apart from our physical isolation from other adults, we often become painfully short of people we can turn to when we crave support. In our pre-mother lives working or studying, we probably had a community of people around us, including allies ever ready to discuss grievances or joke about difficulties. Home alone with children for a large part of the week, we spend less time with other adults. Yet for most of us motherhood is a time when we've never felt more in need of companionship.

Our old friends and family may not understand us; perhaps they don't have children or perhaps their children present different challenges from ours. Parents with sleepless children tend to be surrounded by parents whose children sleep soundly, just as parents with naughty children feel surrounded by parents with placid, well-behaved children. Or maybe when we discuss our problems we find the reactions of our friends and family disappoint us. They may fail to listen effectively: when we raise our worries they might talk about themselves, give us unwelcome advice or change the subject altogether. We may be left feeling unheard, or worse, judged. It's true that other mothers can be great allies, but most of us tend to be poor listeners, if only because our children are constantly interrupting us.

In the event that you know a wise confidant, it's unlikely that this human treasure is available in your times of need. Besides, considerate creatures that we are, mothers are reluctant to burden one person with all our worries, irritations and discomforts.

What about our partners, the people who signed up for the term of this life-long commitment to parenting? In fairness to them, only a saint would be capable of achieving a deep understanding of the physical and psychological challenges we confront. And let's face it, not many of us found ourselves a saint. Even if we did, they'll probably be at work most of the time.

Yes, motherhood forces women into a new kind of self-sufficiency. Our only hope for mothering happily and wisely lies in developing inner resources to nourish ourselves. Tossed around by the needs of others, mothers give and give, so we must find ways to replenish ourselves. The teachings of the Buddha equip us with a multitude of resources for this job, providing us with insights on coping with disturbing emotions and thoughts, as well as on living with others more calmly and happily.

As mothers we're particularly ripe to hear about Buddhism because we have an intimate understanding of two of its cornerstones: we understand there is suffering in life; and we have experienced a truer love.

Who is the Buddha?

The literal meaning of the word Buddha is 'awakened one'. A number of Buddhists throughout history have become 'awakened' and this means there are many Buddhas, past, present and future. Still, when we talk about *the* Buddha, we refer to Siddhartha Gautama born around 560 BC in the Himalayas. His father was one of the many kings in India at that time, but otherwise Siddhartha was an ordinary man with no divine authority.

The life stories of Siddhartha were written down several centuries after his death. Different versions exist, but Buddhists aren't concerned about the lack of an 'authorised version'. In Buddhism the story of the original Buddha is of secondary importance to his message that there is a way out of suffering and unhappiness.

The usual life story you hear goes like this:

> When Siddhartha was born, a holy man prophesied that this newborn would either become a world leader or a great teacher who achieves enlightenment. Preferring the former, his father prevented Siddhartha from experiencing the outside world. Within the palace walls he arranged for his son a stimulating life which included schooling in arts, sciences and sports.
>
> Eventually, some of the servants told Siddhartha about life

outside the palace and triggered his curiosity about the world beyond his walls. Siddhartha started going on excursions and although his father had arranged for the removal of the least fortunate from the streets, Siddhartha came across the aged, the sick, the dead and their grieving relatives. Siddhartha was greatly troubled by the suffering he witnessed and he grew increasingly determined to find out the cause and a way to overcome it. At the age of 29 he abandoned palace life to seek an answer. This meant leaving his wife and his new baby son Rahula (a point about which there is much discussion in Buddhist circles).

For a period of six years, Siddhartha wandered, seeking answers. He experimented with all sorts of practices, including over-indulgence to learn disgust for bodily desires, self-torture, torture inflicted by others, yoga, trances, profound discussion and, finally, fasting. The fasting made him so sick and weak that he broke it and sat down under a tree vowing: 'I will not leave this place until my understanding is complete . . . or I die'. After coming to several realisations on the nature of life, the Buddha became enlightened. Vowing to do what he could to alleviate suffering in the world he spent the remaining 45 years of his life teaching.

The Buddha found the answers through his own efforts and Buddhists are called on to do the same. The Buddha's last words before he died were:

Since there is no external saviour, it is up to each of you to work out your own liberation.

What did the Buddha teach?

The essence of the Buddha's teaching is captured by the four Noble Truths. They all mention suffering, which can be understood to include any unsatisfactoriness, imperfection, anxiety, discomfort, irritation—anything the slightest bit unpleasant. The four Noble Truths are:

1. There is suffering.
2. Attachment causes suffering.
3. Suffering can end.
4. There is a path to end suffering.

So suffering and unsatisfactoriness won't end today, but by embracing some Buddhist practices you can start today planting the seeds to improve your life.

There is suffering—the first Noble Truth

The first of the four Noble Truths of Buddhism is that there is suffering. The Buddha used the word *dukkha*, which best translates as unsatisfactoriness or imperfection. So, the first Noble Truth is that life is inherently unsatisfactory and imperfect. Before motherhood, we may have found this teaching overly pessimistic. If we felt less than happy we could catch a movie, ring a friend or distract ourselves in a myriad ways from any pain. Now our children give us little time to indulge in such distractions. Moreover, we have been through the trials of pregnancy, labour, infants and child raising and hence such a view of life doesn't seem so melodramatic. By now, we have all experienced anguish, even despair.

As mothers we discover life is no light experience. We have responsibilities; pitiable amounts of time to ourselves; desperate worries about whether our children are healthy, 'normal' and able to meet the expectations of the judgemental world around them. We suffer guilt that we're not attending to the hundred other things we could be doing. We agonise over our careers and, in many cases, the loss thereof. In our darker moments we may struggle for self-esteem as we watch the worry lines set in and our body parts begin to point down.

Many mothers remark on how having children changes their experience of watching the nightly news. As mothers, we feel the pain in the world more. We now see victims of crimes, wars and drug addiction as the precious children of suffering mothers. Stories of kidnappings, child abuse or suicide feel like more than we can bear. We understand that any death or loss affects a vulnerable family unit. Our reactions are a sign of our deepened awareness of suffering and unsatisfactoriness in life.

Part of the cause of unsatisfactoriness is what Buddhists call **impermanence**, or the way that everything must change into something else—nothing stays the same. Everything in life—people, circumstances, objects down to the smallest particle—is in process, and this leaves us with nothing solid and lasting to rely on. Buddhism doesn't deny that happiness is possible, for it is. The problem is that we can't hold onto happiness. As with everything, it passes. A life typically includes birth, ageing, pain and death. We can spend our lives distracting ourselves from these facts but they are inescapable.

You may agree that life has its elements of suffering, but who wants to dwell on these? Buddhism could look like a depressing path if this was as far as you investigated. Happily, the next three Noble Truths present the good news; but for now, if you wanted a summary of what Buddhism is about, take it from the Buddha:

> *I teach suffering and the end of suffering.*

The mind of love

The second reason mothers are ripe to benefit from Buddhism is that we've taken an enormous step towards attaining what Buddhists call 'the mind of love'. As we know, motherhood is about far more than suffering; it's also about a mind-expanding experience of love.

The love of a mother for a child is the truest love around. Loving a child teaches us what real love is: selfless, patient and forgiving. We learn that love is unconditional, non-judgemental and expects little if anything in return. Of course there are times when we resent our children, when they put us in touch with the dark sides of our natures, but overall our relationship with them is one of overwhelming love. As one mother puts it:

> After I had a child I realised that all the love I had experienced in the past—especially with partners—was selfish. I was constantly thinking, what's in this relationship for me? And if my expectations weren't met any good feeling would dry up altogether. My daughter has taken me to hell and back but there's nothing she can do to make me stop loving her.

Our love for our children brings us joy, bliss and happiness. What's really inspiring though, is that through loving a child we deepen our capacity to be a loving person for others too. The potential to take what we learn from loving our child and apply it to other relationships is limitless. Many mothers discover this for themselves: they feel more compassion towards other human beings, realising they all started as precious babies worthy of a mother's devotion. These mothers discover a new potential to be patient with the surly cashier, the aggressive driver or the needy relation.

I once took part in a Buddhist course about developing loving kindness in relationships. When giving an example of true love, the teacher always referred to the love of a mother for a child. She used the mother–child relationship to demonstrate how love makes us behave as well as the benefits that true love brings. I feel privileged that as a mother I can understand such teaching from first-hand experience.

For me, the most accurate comment on motherhood is that it makes your life twice as bad *and* twice as good. There is suffering and unsatisfactoriness, but love saves us.

Gentle, patient and persistent

Another reason mothers are ripe to hear some Buddhist teachings is that they can be so mercilessly demanding of themselves. Many mothers strive to meet the highest standards and expectations of their role only to feel guilty for failing to be the perfect mother, partner, relation, friend, worker, housekeeper, dieter and citizen. So, at a time in our lives when we need support and compassion, we criticise ourselves. Most of us wouldn't dream of talking to others as harshly as we berate ourselves.

Buddhism teaches compassion for all living beings and this must include ourselves. Although Buddhism calls for high standards of behaviour it doesn't require us to waste our energy on feeling guilty—we avoid self-recrimination as unhelpful. When our thoughts and actions are less than wise, all we need is to be aware, to pay attention rather than let them forge ahead unnoticed. We aim to see clearly what is going on. And we actively cultivate more healthy states of mind.

I once heard a meditation teacher advise: 'You needn't become frustrated if your mind wanders during mediation—your approach should be *gentle, patient* and *persistent.*' I immediately memorised those words for I could see their value both for meditation and for daily life. To nourish our self-sufficiency, we need to become our own best friends and when we feel like we haven't met our standards remember to be *gentle, patient* and *persistent* with ourselves, as this mother has found:

> One of the greatest gifts of Buddhism for me is its emphasis on patience and compassion for yourself. Raised in a very Catholic home, as a teenager I would torture myself with guilt for failing to overcome sin. No matter how hard I tried I couldn't stop sinning and ended up feeling defeated and liking myself less. Buddhism required me to become aware of my weaknesses on a deep level. Rather than crushing them on

sight, I had to first understand where they were coming from, or what was causing them.

For example, one of my weaknesses is a tendency to be judgemental of others. Buddhism taught me that if I could be aware of the judgements I was making, the thought processes behind them and their effect on my mind and body, then my awareness would give me a much greater chance of becoming more compassionate towards others. There's no need to get angry with myself or feel guilty. I have learned to be more patient and forgiving with myself and this has been a far more effective way to deal with my flaws than punishing myself with guilt.

I teach my children how to behave from a base of love and unconditional acceptance. I'm now learning to do the same for myself.

What can Buddhism offer mothers?

Imagine a calm, serene mother, who accepts whatever life presents her with. Unexpected or unwanted events don't rattle her. She never overreacts. She's aware of the times when she lacks wisdom or compassion but she doesn't waste days feeling guilty, she might do better next time. She's self-aware, but because she has fostered self-love, she is not self-conscious or self-absorbed when she talks to others. Her friends say she is gentle and kind in a genuine way. Her brothers and sisters add that she is clear in her thinking and good at making decisions. She seems to make others feel comfortable, special even, and there's no shortage of people who love her. Her children delight in her company for she makes them feel important and understood. She's creative, spontaneous and quick to laugh because no matter what she's doing, life is play, not work.

Buddhism can help us to become more like this mother, a happier kind of mother. It takes time, but with compassion and patience for ourselves—as opposed to self-recrimination and guilt-mongering—we move a little closer to this ideal as our practice deepens. It's not that Buddhism will create a mass of clone-like Perfect Mothers—there are many millions of ways to be like this mother and still fulfil your own unique purpose.

What do Buddhist mothers say?

One significant effect that practising Buddhism can have on our life is that we might actually be there for it. As our life unfolds, rather than being mentally elsewhere, as we usually are, we strive to be present in the here and now. Chapter 2 explores this idea in more depth, but let's hear what a few Buddhist mothers have to say about the effect of Buddhist teachings on their day-to-day life.

Anne, the mother of two young daughters:

> Buddhism helps me to see motherhood as a spiritual journey. At the worst of times, I can remind myself that parenting is practice and practice of the most rigorous kind. My children are my teachers repeatedly forcing me to live in the present moment and give up fantasising about all the exciting and stimulating things I *could* be doing.
>
> As a mother you constantly need to ask the questions: 'What does this moment require?' and 'What is important here?' On bad days I notice my daughters automatically repeating themselves as though they know I'm a distant zombie who's not quite there with them. When this happens I know to yank myself back into the present and give them close attention. Following Buddhist teachings I'm likely to parent *consciously* and with awareness of what the present moment requires rather than allowing my children to become the victims of my automatic reactions.

In *Why Buddhism? Westerners in Search of Wisdom*, a book of interviews with practising Buddhists, Vicki Mackenzie interviews an

American mother, Yvonne Rand, who is also a Zen priest and a teacher. Yvonne echoes Anne's sentiment that parenting can be spiritual practice.

> The meditation helped me with my parenting, although my kids were aware of it more than myself. Once when my daughter was visiting a schoolmate the mother asked, 'Why does your mother meditate?' and my daughter's response was, 'Well, she's nicer to be around and it looks like she feels better.' It was quite accurate. One of the effects for me was like waking up after being for a long time in a slumber state. I began to see how much I'd been on automatic. I also felt I'd found home . . .
>
> It became abundantly clear to me that if my relationship with my children was not consistent with what I was studying in Buddhism then in some way I was being a fraud. I was interested in using my relationship with my children as an opportunity for studying my own mind stream, and cultivating self-awareness. I could see that my state of mind had a big effect on my kids.

Melissa has two young daughters aged three and five. She too uses Buddhism to gain control over her emotions. Without becoming complacent, Melissa seems to have achieved a measure of self-acceptance.

> Buddhism has helped me become more conscious of the workings of my mind. Whenever I can remember, I try to be aware of how I'm talking to myself. This requires attention and concentration which I develop in meditation.
>
> These days, through increased awareness of my mental mutterings, I try to catch myself being negative. On a bad day with the kids, so much of my thinking is complaining and working myself into a state of despair. When you develop the ability to watch this process you are better able to challenge your perceptions and save yourself from suffering.

We see in all these examples, that when we bring a clear and grounded mind to the challenges in our day, we are more likely to respond constructively.

Insurance against parenting nightmares

Personally, I want to be ready for any testing times in the future, especially my sons' adolescence. I want to have the inner resources that will make me an asset to their lives, whether it be as a friend, confidant or someone capable of minding their own business when necessary. Like most mothers my greatest fear is that my precious babies might one day suffer. In dark moments, I torment myself with images of their experiencing loneliness, depression or humiliation. And should either of them commit suicide I see myself perishing from grief.

My intuition tells me the wiser I am, the more approachable I'll be and the greater chance I'll have of helping my children when they're in distress. If my children respect me they're more likely to confide in me. They may struggle to respect me if they see me as out-of-touch with myself, unable to control my emotions or lacking in compassion. They certainly wouldn't share their worries with someone they saw as set in rigid opinions. By making us more self-aware, practising Buddhism helps us gradually peel away the less skilful layers of our characters and this makes us more approachable for our children when they suffer.

Although the children of skilful parents can still find their way into trouble, with wiser parents the scope for our children to experience misery must decline. As the Dalai Lama put it in *The Heart of Buddha's Path*: 'When parents are warm-hearted, peaceful and calm people, generally speaking their children will also develop that attitude and behaviour.'

Practising Buddhism can make us wiser and, if only for the sake of my children, wise is what I aspire to be. But what is wisdom? When our children are in distress they aren't necessarily looking for an expert or an authority. They might not want us to provide answers from our reading, our experiences or our travels. In Buddhism wisdom is not about making judgements and knowing the answers. Accepting the mystery in life, refusing to jump to our usual automatic conclusions, a humble attitude of not-knowing—these are what help us to be open and sensitive in all our interactions.

The cause of suffering—the second Noble Truth

As mothers most of us have had some experience of discomfort or anguish, so the first Noble Truth is relatively easy to understand and accept. The second Noble Truth is more of a revelation. It explains that the cause of suffering and unsatisfactoriness is desire. The world we live in has turned us into creatures tormented by innumerable desires. The objects of our desire won't bring us peace and we are often blind to the effects of our endless striving for them.

We desire to be somebody important, to be admired, to make our fortune, to have endless sources of excitement. We obsessively pursue our goals, telling ourselves that our lives will be all fixed up once we achieve them. We collect masses of stuff because we yearn to be fashionable, tasteful, 'up there' or 'out there', anywhere but *here*. Although we see our desires as stepping stones on the way to happiness, they in fact make us overlook any potential for happiness in the present moment.

Adrienne Howley, an Australian Buddhist nun ordained by the Dalai Lama in 1982 and mother of two, was chatting to one of her sons:

> I was bemoaning, not for the first time, the fact that no matter what one did for or gave to my mother she was never satisfied. She would take it, of course, but left no doubt that it was the wrong colour or shape or not what she had really wanted. I said that she did not seem to know what she wanted. My son smiled and said quietly, 'Mother, you don't understand her.

> That's all. She *does* know what she wants—she just wants *everything*.' We are all a bit like that and some of us throw spectacular tantrums when we can't have it all, and suffer exceedingly and cause others to suffer also.

A life free from desire doesn't mean a life without effort, aspirations or even wishes. The suffering starts when we turn our goals or preferences into demands or needs: to be happy I must have *x*, *y* and *z*. By craving and insisting on what we want, we pave the way for feelings of anxiety and frustration when what we want is not forthcoming. Even when our desires are fulfilled, we don't find lasting happiness—we come up with some more desires.

We suffer from desires for what we don't have, but we also suffer from desires to not have what we have. Aversion, the flipside of attachment, has the same power to create unhappiness and is especially relevant for mothers. Standing in a park, your child refuses to come home. You've been there for what seems like hours. You feel cold and hungry. Waves of frustration and helplessness course through your body as you try to persuade the wee rebel to come home.

Or this one. It's been raining for days. You haven't had enough sleep and you've been stuck in your noisy living room for hours. Your children have been arguing, nagging and forcing you to listen to their awful music. You lose your temper over some spilt juice, then think to yourself, 'I hate this. I can't be a mother! It's all been a dreadful mistake!' Aversion.

Rather than battling individually with each of our attachments, the Buddha claimed there was one attachment which caused all the others and if you could deal with this one the others would fade away: *our belief in a solid, separate and consistent self, an ego*. Our ego turns us into lifelong slaves, propping up our fragile self-image, seeking pleasure and avoiding pain. This life-changing revelation is explored in Chapter 9.

Suffering can end— the third Noble Truth

Across the Buddhist schools there are many definitions and explanations of enlightenment and the end of suffering. Enlightenment comes when our minds are completely purified of negative states. No longer ignorant, we become delusion-free. Seeing the truth clearly, we know to stop chasing pleasure and avoiding pain. Our hearts fill with love as we have conquered selfishness. In the Zen school, enlightenment is available to us in any moment. Other schools claim it takes several lifetimes and that there are several stages. It's generally agreed though that to finally awaken is something that words can't capture and the unenlightened mind can't comprehend. All schools also agree that responsibility for achieving enlightenment lies with the individual—there's no saviour or magic power that decides when we're ready.

On achieving enlightenment while meditating under his tree, the Buddha said:

> *Everything is extraordinarily clear. I see the whole landscape before me. I see my hands, my feet, my toes and I smell the rich river mud. I feel a sense of tremendous strangeness and wonder at being alive. Wonder of wonders! This enlightenment is the nature of all people but they are unhappy for the lack of it.*

In meditation it's possible to achieve glimpses of the enlightened mind, that spur us on. Such an experience is achievable at the highest levels of concentration and is likely to take years to reach. As the fourth Noble Truth prescribes, it's a matter of following the path.

The path out of suffering— the fourth Noble Truth

The Buddha explained the path out of suffering and unhappiness, the fourth Noble Truth, by way of the Noble Eightfold Path, with its three parts: wisdom, ethics and mental discipline. We find that any Buddhist teaching falls into one of these eight categories.

Wisdom
1. Skilful Understanding
2. Skilful Thought

Ethics
3. Skilful Speech
4. Skilful Action
5. Skilful Livelihood

Mental Discipline
6. Skilful Effort
7. Skilful Mindfulness
8. Skilful Concentration

Skilful Understanding is about seeing life the way it is; particularly, that we understand the truths of impermanence, unsatisfactoriness and no-self. **Skilful Thought** is about having a serious attitude to Buddhist practice, a determination to increase your awareness and purify your thoughts from greed, hatred and delusion.

Skilful Speech, **Action** and **Livelihood** give the path its moral base. We need to speak, act and make our living in a way that shows compassion, loving kindness and fairness to others. The path to wisdom requires that we live ethically. In Buddhism, only those who live with integrity can fully enjoy the fruits of meditation.

Skilful Effort, **Mindfulness** and **Concentration** relate to meditation practice, and we investigate these in later chapters.

For now this explanation is probably enough detail to digest. You can find a more thorough explanation of the Noble Eightfold Path in Appendix 1 and some of the categories are discussed in later chapters.

CHAPTER 2

parenting mindfully

I LOVE PICKING ZAC up from childcare at the end of a day. The delicious anticipation as I walk from the car and through the centre, seeing his face light up when he notices me, dissolving into his welcoming hug—this is a joyful experience where my mind is completely engaged in the present moment.

The next day at home with him I find myself restless and irritable or lethargic from the slowness of time. In such a state I can be blind to how exquisite he looks, his hilarious remarks, and the sheer miracle that his life is. He is a blessing, an extraordinary gift. By watching him more closely as often as possible and studying who he has become in each new moment, I afford myself a richer and more satisfying experience of motherhood.

If we could learn to live in full awareness of our present moment and explore our own 'nowness', instead of rehashing the past or planning the future, we would find more joy in our lives, even moments of unsurpassed bliss. This is mindfulness, the seventh category of the Eightfold Path, a path that leads us out of suffering and into happiness. The term 'mindfulness' can be misleading, suggesting a mind that is full. Rather, mindfulness is *knowing what's happening at the time it's happening*.

We tend to charge through our days on automatic pilot. Preoccupied with our thoughts, we perform our tasks through a mental haze. Our thoughts rebound back and forth between a version of the past and plans for the future. Our consciousness buzzes with past conflicts, hurtful remarks and regrets, along with fantasies, daydreams and to-do lists. It's quite possible for us to reach the end of a day to find that we have effectively missed the whole thing, and have no idea what actually happened. Having spent the day in our own heads we may have failed to:

- focus on our tasks
- listen attentively to our children
- taste more than the first bite of our food
- notice our surroundings

- feel any build-up of tension in our bodies
- acknowledge our emotions and what triggered them.

Practising mindfulness will make us wiser as parents. Only with mindfulness in the present moment do we have any hope of understanding the true nature of things, or 'what is'. Without this understanding we are left to perceive our lives through the clouds of our delusions. With mindfulness we can develop clear-sightedness.

To bring awareness to each moment of the day is enormously difficult. With our 'monkey minds' which dart back and forth between memories and plans, we will drift from the present over a hundred times each day. Why not run on automatic? Surely there would need to be numerous benefits in mindfulness for us to bother, for us to accept the countless and inevitable failures to pay attention.

Mindfulness—for our children's sake

How mindful are we in our most important role as parents? To what extent are we missing their childhoods by not paying attention in the present moment? I spoke to one mother who understands the importance of mindful parenting from experiencing a childhood without it.

> I've always felt sad and confused about my relationship with my parents. They were great parents—you couldn't fault them really, and I feel enormously grateful to them. The trouble in my family though is that we're all a bit vague and scatty. We don't have great attention spans and this has meant that we've never listened to each other and so we've never really known or understood each other. Although Mum has always been there for me, when I speak to her she interrupts, changes the subject, isn't really tuning in or gives me the same old response she's always given without really hearing what I've said. I hate

> to sound like a big victim when my suffering is so much less than that of, say, neglected children, but I just can't deny the sad feeling that comes from never feeling properly noticed or understood.
>
> Buddhism has taught me that the whole problem boils down to a lack of mindfulness, an inability to be quiet and still for each other, to regard each other with attention, patience and openness. At least I can learn from the mistakes of my family and try to be more present for my own children. I want to provide them—and my husband—with moments of full attention, engagement and connection, so that they are not left with what my Zen teacher calls 'a missing experience'.

This mother's words have stayed with me for I sense the danger inherent in her story. On days when my practice of mindfulness is weak and I'm miles away from my present moment, I might realise that Zac has asked me the same question two or three times before I snap to attention. I notice many children doing this with the adults in their life and I see the potential for children to feel unimportant, ignored or invisible. We all do it and there's no need to beat ourselves up about it, only the need to be aware of it and do our best to overcome it. Now I try to treat Zac's voice as an 'ON' switch for my practice of mindfulness. Sometimes I have to nudge his father and other friends and relations, 'Zac's just asking you something.'

Our children bring to our lives an abundance of special moments: their birth, their first smile, their first word, starting school. But caught up in a fast-flowing stream of thoughts we miss so many of the more everyday moments and, indeed, the potential for every moment we spend with our children to be special. Awake to the depth and texture of the present, we open ourselves to appreciate and enjoy them more.

Living in awareness of the present moment, our families will be safer as we diminish the scope for careless minor accidents along with the chances of driving into the back of a truck. We are also able to be more sensitive to what our children need from us, as this mother puts it:

> I find when I parent inattentively I can react to my children in destructive ways. When I look deeply into the moment and see what it asks of me, I can help my children sensitively. In my tradition, Zen, we speak of 'Beginner's Mind', where you see each new moment with fresh eyes rather than falling back on the same old reactions. I find this very helpful for parenting: what worked today might not work tomorrow, just as our way of dealing with one child might not work dealing with another. So I try to respond to exactly what this new moment presents. Parenthood is nothing if not unpredictable so I need to respond differently to each new situation seeing each instant for what it is.

And this mother points out that with mindfulness we become more aware of who our children are and more able to free them from any pressure to fulfil unrealistic expectations.

> With awareness I see my children for who they are and free them from the chains of my expectations and fears. This way they can develop in their own way. I'll resist pressuring my daughter to become a philosophical ballet dancer who helps the sick, loves animals and idolises her mother. Attuned to her interests I can help her to achieve her goals which are likely to differ from what I had expected.

Mindfulness—for our own sake

As this mother found, mindfulness also allows us to learn more about ourselves and we discover that in so many ways our children 'raise' us.

> Awareness of the present moment teaches me about myself and enables time spent with my children to be a time of learning and spiritual growth—often it's a case of learning from my mistakes, but a time of learning all the same. After I fly off the handle, or snap at the kids, I could choose to distract myself from the discomfort as soon as possible, to escape the unpleasant present. Instead I try to look deeply into the moment for what I should be learning and how I can improve my reaction for next time those same buttons get pushed.
>
> By watching my thoughts I've learned so much about the unrealistic demands I make on my children and my living conditions in general. Silly things like 'the house must be tidy' or 'my children must always be happy or grateful'. I've learned the need to be more emotionally detached from all those petty irritations, to settle for imperfection.

And on a lighter note, this mother who strives to keep her mind in the present notices fewer bruises.

> I used to rush around with a mind always stressing about the future. I never seemed to have my mind on what I was doing in the moment and as a result I was always bumping into things, hitting my toes on furniture, whacking my hips on tables. Since I've started giving more attention to the moment, the here and now, I've stopped hurting myself.

Mindfulness is an awareness of all the present moment contains: the sensations of your body, your feelings, perceptions, assumptions and tendencies. We notice the sensations in our bodies and we might see that a dark mood comes more from the hunger in our stomach or the ache in our neck than from our children's behaviour. We might also take more care of our bodies as we learn which foods truly satisfy us, which positions feel most comfortable or how much better we feel after exercise. How are we breathing—shallowly, quickly? How relaxed are our muscles: where is the tension and what is causing it? What is our posture like and what does this say about our state of mind?

Being able to observe the rising and passing away of our emotions with mindfulness ensures we experience our lives fully, never ignoring the issues that can teach us the most. Interestingly, we can find ourselves complaining bitterly about some grievance but on looking more deeply discover that it's not the grievance that is really bothering us. Rather, we are in the grip of some transient emotion and we use the grievance to justify it. Call it a bad mood or blame 'something I ate', it's useful to be keenly aware of this tendency so that we don't exaggerate the seriousness of grievances and overreact to them.

Late in the afternoon with children I often find myself experiencing thoughts along the lines of, 'motherhood is driving me mad, I need to escape, I'm not cut out for this lifestyle'. When I catch myself thinking this way, it helps to remember that I'm in the grip of a transient emotion for which I need to come up with some grievances. Frantically seeking justification for my low ebb, I fabricate catastrophes and frustrations. How easily I forget that this is just my usual late afternoon blues: my sugar levels are low, I'm tired and ready for a break. These feelings have little to do with motherhood, for back in my pre-motherhood days of full-time work I used to think in the same way at this time of the day: I'd exaggerate the difficulties of the job and fantasise about freedom before ducking out for some chocolate relief. So it's always worth asking myself, what came first: the emotion or the grievance?

It's also useful to ask ourselves how our emotions affect our body sensations. When I feel angry with my children, I frown, tense my right shoulder and breathe unevenly. If I can catch myself in this state I can exercise some self-control by addressing the bodily tension first, releasing it, breathing more deeply and calming myself down.

'Now' offers not only perceptions of your inner world but awareness of your surroundings too, using all your senses: the feel of the air on your skin, the crunch of leaves underfoot, the view, the sounds, the smells. Challenging ourselves to notice our surroundings we may be surprised at how many of the details of our neighbourhood we have overlooked. We tend to walk along, heads down, absorbed in our own thoughts or noticing only a narrow set of all there is to perceive. Often we rely on our children to point out the details of our landscape. How many beautiful sights, sounds and smells are we missing out on because we don't notice? Consciously noticing my surroundings I have learned how melancholy, how touching the sounds of birds singing can be. As I push the pram through the streets, I notice flowers, trees, rocks, the interplay of colour, the gentle movement of clouds. Joy needn't always come from life's big, splashy events.

Mindfulness enriches our lives further still by giving us more energy, calmness and insight.

Energy

In our daily lives we waste energy by failing to be focussed on the present moment and what it requires: we make mistakes, say things we regret and get distracted from our tasks. Born in Britain, Helen Jandamit is a Buddhist mother with two sons. For over 20 years she has been teaching meditation at the International Buddhist Meditation Centre in Bangkok. In her book *The Path to Peace Within*, she adopts a useful analogy to illustrate how we find more energy:

> Imagine you are holding a bowl which is completely full of water. If you walk along with concentrated attention, very little water will spill. But if you walk along with jerky, uncontrolled movements, a lot of water will be lost.

Mindfulness saves energy and time. With poor concentration, we need to repeat some of our actions because we didn't perform them mindfully the first time. An unclear mind may cause you to forget where you put things, why you came into a room, whether you locked the car, even your train of thought mid-conversation. Mindfulness counteracts absent-mindedness and cultivates mental sharpness.

Our energy levels rise for a number of reasons. Not least, mindfulness ensures we are in good form more often and this happier state of mind allows us to enjoy more energy and less lethargy. Additionally, the mental stillness experienced in meditation increases energy levels enough for many experienced meditators to claim they need less sleep.

By being more aware of how our body is responding to the events of the day, we can conserve our energy. As one Buddhist mother puts it:

> As often as I can, I try to be mindful of how my body is feeling and this pays off. Whenever I bring my awareness to my body, I notice tension. By regularly releasing this tension and reminding myself to relax, I finish the day with more energy than if I had let the tension build up.
>
> I also tend to tighten my facial muscles throughout the day. In becoming aware of this I know it's time to smile and take things more lightly. I'm sure that relaxing my face helps my relationships as well—people are less likely to catch me glaring at them.

Calmness

Through meditation and mindful living we enjoy a mental holiday from our usual round of thoughts, worries and plans. As with any holiday, this refreshes us so we feel more peaceful and the challenges we face become less overwhelming. Living mindfully we feel happier; how could we not when we willingly let go of all the preoccupations that keep us from noticing any joy in the present moment? We start to experience the 'here and now' more richly.

In meditation we have a chance to practise dealing with negative emotions and we can transfer this ability to our daily lives. We come to understand that negative emotions are transient mental states so we needn't become too caught up in them. There's no need to express, suppress or act on them. Noticing the point at which a negative mood arises helps us to pause before we respond. With more awareness of our negative emotions, we increase our chances of bringing them under control and living with calmness.

Sitting in traffic we catch ourselves growing irritable: we acknowledge the feeling, watch it develop, have being, and eventually pass away. By mindfully observing our growing impatience with a grizzling child, we have found a way to avoid identifying with the emotion too closely. We pause to collect ourselves so that we can respond in a manner that feels wise and thoughtful.

Today, practising mindfulness saved me from 'losing it'. I had friends from interstate staying and I really wanted them to feel at home. My baby had a temperature, was screaming and insisting that I carry him. My son Zac had a tantrum or four and had been yelling at one of the smaller guests—who was taking it badly. A plumber had turned off our water. We were out of milk.

Determined to bring the benefits of mindfulness to my situation, I observed my inner world throughout the morning. Adopting a 'noticing' attitude, I observed negative thought heaped on negative thought (Not this! . . . I should've known that would happen! . . . This is unbelievable!), and negative emotion heaped on negative emotion (frustration, exasperation and plenty of good old anger). I knew that if I identified too closely with my negative emotions—stopped watching them and started giving in to them—I'd sink (and possibly wallop someone, hopefully not the plumber). And whenever I could, I tried to pay attention to my breathing to keep myself grounded.

I was aware of a very clear choice: I could allow all the mini-catastrophes to turn me into a quivering wreck or I could choose a spacious response of relative detachment (What would any of this matter by tomorrow anyway?). I tried to accept the situation rather than wasting energy on aversion and resistance. As mothers we won't always be comfortable and relaxed but we can still foster an attitude of tolerance for our situation, telling ourselves that every moment is part of our spiritual practice. In the Zen tradition, there is a saying,

'The whole world is medicine'. We can learn from everything that happens to us. We look more closely at how mindfulness helps us cope with negative mind states in the next chapter.

Insight

Thinking and talking at a rational or intellectual level will not always allow us a way out of our delusions, bad habits and worst tendencies. Many of us have been in relationships where we tried to fix problems by talking about them. If this didn't work what did we do? We talked some more and still nothing was resolved. We have had the same experience with thinking through our problems: too often, the more we think the more we tie ourselves in knots. Sometimes we need something more powerful to transform our experience.

We need insight or an ability to see a problem with clarity. Insights, or realisations, can occur automatically if we are mindful and develop our ability to see what is truly going on. When we finally see and understand the misconceptions underlying our self-defeating behaviour it's only natural to start behaving differently.

One Buddhist mother I interviewed had consulted a Zen therapist about feelings of guilt. For her, one of the more difficult aspects of motherhood is the lack of recognition and attention. She felt embarrassed about her desire for some limelight and adulation. Rather than rely on intellectual discussion alone, the therapist used mindfulness techniques to stimulate understanding and insights on a deeper level. As the mother explains:

> First, we discussed the complexities of my feelings around this issue of recognition. Then she took the issue to a deeper level, asking me to close my eyes and concentrate on my body sensations, on my breath and on anything arising in the present moment. Quietly, she told me that she was going to say one thing and leave me to sit with it for a minute or two, in quietness.
>
> Then she said it.
>
> 'It's OK to be noticed.'

I sat in stillness letting it sink in without so much *thinking* about it as being with it. And I have to say that after an hour-long session with her it is this one statement—it's OK to be noticed—that has stayed with me rather than anything we spoke about at an intellectual level. That one statement has been very healing for me as it helps me to accept myself and forgive myself for being such a needy show-off.

Developing mindfulness

Any one moment is bursting with hundreds of details both within us and around us. The challenge lies in remembering to remember or in paying attention. In meditation and during our day, we fall victim to thoughts and impulses that distract us from being mindful. Even though our thoughts are so often unhelpful, we become caught up in our inner dramas. In remembering to remember, we never condemn ourselves when our mind wanders but patiently draw our attention back to the present moment. This doesn't mean we empty our minds and become thought-free zombies. The present, no matter what we are doing, is always full enough to occupy our mind.

No movement or gesture is too small for mindfulness. To quote the Buddha:

> *. . . a monk knows when he is going, 'I am going.' He knows when he is standing, 'I am standing.' He knows when he is sitting, 'I am sitting.' He knows he is lying down, 'I am lying down.'*

This monk is making 'mental acknowledgements'. Although it feels strange at first, telling yourself what you are doing as you are doing it, is a way to hold onto mindfulness. It's like using training wheels to learn to ride a bike. Eventually you may no longer need them as you improve your ability to become one with the present moment.

In noticing the details of the present moment we need to avoid rating them 'good' or 'bad', 'pleasant' or 'unpleasant'. The Buddhist aims for a still mind which can neither be rattled or overexcited by what it sees, like the stillness of a mountain weathering the extremities of each passing season. Refusing to rate what we perceive helps us to cultivate feelings of acceptance rather than judgement, as we stop demanding that life be other than it is. This is the quality of equanimity, so highly prized by Buddhists. Refusing to rate what we perceive also helps us to avoid the self-condemnation and guilt that afflict so many mothers. We don't need to be left feeling inadequate about our performance.

Over the next few days as you go about your life, challenge yourself to live in the present moment. Be conscious of your body sensations and the rise and fall of emotional states. Try to observe your thoughts rather than let them run off on their own course. See how often your mind travels into the past and future, how much persistence it takes to keep it grounded in the Now.

You are likely to find your attempts to stay in the present moment very humbling—few can do it for long! We need to train our minds so that we can eventually pay attention for longer stretches of time. We increase our capacity for mindfulness by meditating, a time to practise concentrating on one aspect of the present moment—usually the rise and fall of the breath. In Chapter 9 we explore mindfulness meditations which allow us to work on our concentration skills and increase our potential to experience joy in the present moment. But aside from meditation, we can practise mindfulness at any moment; every second of the day is an opportunity to be mindful: eating, drinking, waiting, resting, talking, working . . .

Living mindfully when you're time-poor

You may have a new baby, a sleep-deprived life or the juggle of work and kids. Even if you are time-poor, or even time-bankrupt, mindfulness can still bring enormous benefits to your life. You may have next to no time for meditation but you have every waking second available to cultivate mindfulness. The challenge is to remember to remember.

A meditation teacher in California and author of *Living Meditation, Living Insight*, Dr Thynn Thynn believes that sitting in meditation is merely an aid and shouldn't become more important than living meditatively in daily experience. She argues that meditation needs to be a 'dynamic activity' that we tie into the daily chaos.

> Meditation is here and now, amid the ups and downs of life, amidst conflicts, disappointments, heartaches, joys, success and stress of living. It is amidst the chaos that we need to practise mindfulness to find peace within ourselves and the end of our suffering.

She suggests that we use all the stimuli around us to root our minds in the moment.

> The practice of living meditation is not to run away or disregard the distractions but to use these distractions themselves as our focus to practise mindfulness.

Tenzin Palmo, the English Buddhist nun who spent 12 years meditating in a cave, claims in *Cave in the Snow* that everyone has time to meditate:

> You can meditate walking down the corridor, waiting for the computer to change, at the traffic lights, standing in a queue, going to the bathroom, combing your hair. Just be there in the present, without the mental commentary.

She suggests we start by choosing one action we do daily, such as drinking tea, during which to meditate.

Kamala Masters received the same advice from her teacher. These days Kamala is a co-director of the Vipassana Metta Foundation in

Maui, Hawaii. In *Voices of Insight* Kamala recounts how, as a young mother longing to walk a spiritual path, she felt frustrated by her complete lack of time: she was a single mother with three kids and two jobs. Never giving up, she met a teacher who visited her home. He identified two opportunities for meditation. First, she was to meditate while washing the dishes.

> Have a general awareness of just washing the dishes, the movement of your hands, the warmth or coolness of the water, picking a dish up, soaping it, rinsing it, putting it down. Nothing else is happening now—just washing the dishes.

Her teacher also noticed that many times a day she walked down the hallway. He advised her, whenever she was in the hall, to:

> . . . use the time as an opportunity to be present with the simple act of walking . . . With each step, very quietly in your mind you can note, 'stepping, stepping, stepping'.

This short time, several times a day, helped Kamala to live more calmly with her children. Before long she was extending the mindfulness to more household chores and observing all the benefits that come from meditation practice. In Zen monasteries chores are an important opportunity for practice and in some monasteries the most menial work is allocated to the more senior members.

Here are some ways to cultivate mindfulness in our daily lives:

- When you walk, say to yourself, 'I am walking', and feel the effects of the ground on your feet.
- When you do housework, notice every detail of the task.
- When you eat, be conscious of the movements of your hands, the taste of the food, the sensations of swallowing and digesting, the feel of the food in your stomach.

- When you wait, in a bank queue or at the supermarket, pay attention to all the sensations of your body. Do you need to relax tense muscles, correct your posture or soften your face?
- Wherever you are, take in your surroundings. Challenge yourself to notice a new detail about your neighbourhood every day.
- Listen attentively to others and pause before jumping into the conversation.
- Watch your thinking processes as often as possible and without judgemental comment.
- Take every opportunity to focus on your breathing to rest your mind.
- Seek opportunities for silence and stillness. Sometimes it makes sense to resist the car radio, the TV or idle chatter.

I can also recommend what I call the 'one-minute grab'. During a full day with children, you occasionally find time to yourself which typically lasts about one minute. I often use this time to practise mindfulness of the breath and am constantly amazed at the results that even one minute of focussing on the rise and fall of my breath can achieve. It's calming and somehow leaves you feeling more positive. Curiously, such a transformation can happen even when my concentration is not sharp. I find the effects are enhanced if during this short meditation I adopt the classic half-grin of the Buddha.

I have tried to make time for more formal sitting meditation too. Soon after my second baby arrived, I had to find time for moving house, starting renovations (my husband's idea!) and finishing this book. Finding time for sitting meditation was a great challenge, but I did manage to fit a few short sittings into my week. Most of them were around six o'clock in the morning after feeding the baby and almost all of them were interrupted by the pull of domestic life. I was fortunate at this time to catch a talk by Tibetan Lama Choedak, a father of three. He made the point that practice and parenting should be as one and that we needn't compartmentalise one from the other. If your child cries when you are halfway through your meditation, your concentration needs to flow smoothly, without resistance and mental comment, to what is required of you in that moment: comforting your baby. In his own words:

> The carry-over of the practice is more important than the formal practice itself. The time you use the petrol is not at the petrol pump.

As slaves to time, we can live with an obsession for 'getting stuff done', for building and achieving. When we slip too far into this way of thinking, we end up fitting our children in around our own arrangements and becoming less sensitive to their needs. We can't enjoy our children because our minds are elsewhere. When focussed on the present, we free ourselves to become open to the potential of the moment, to simply 'be'. Susan Murphy is a Zen teacher and mother of two who speaks of mindfulness as 'the gateway out of the steel teeth of time':

> The child offers a constant invitation into presence and into play. And you can't play with a child unless you're prepared to be completely present. A creative energy of playfulness grows in us as we grow into our practice. Think of going for a walk with a young child, how incredibly long it takes to cover a block—so many things you have to look at, to comment on and ask questions about. Looking down into a puddle, you discover it's actually like a mirror. Is it a mirror or is it a window? Is that us we see in that puddle or is it another world? It looks different to this world. I remember when my daughter was five or six we had to stop every time we saw moss and we had to walk our fingers through the fairy world like fairies—the little tiny clumps of moss were like fairy trees. So walks were very long, and time was very long. It's like the child elongates time till it starts to dissolve. They don't live in our tick-tock time. They force you to put aside for a while your usual goal-oriented behaviour. And that's an extraordinary gift and teaching.

Karma

Once your children are grown, what kind of mother will you have been? How will your children describe you? A martyr? Patient? Crabby? Demanding? Easy-going? What effect will our words and actions have had on our children? And what kind of model will we have provided? In Buddhism, it's often said that if you want an explanation for your present look at your past; if you want to know your future look at your present. We can't change our past nor dictate our future; all we can influence is the present moment, so that's where we need to invest our awareness. This is why mindfulness is so important: it affects our future and, of course, our children's.

There needn't be anything magical or superstitious in our understanding of karma. The way the Buddha described it, it sounds perfectly logical. It's not about the universe making judgements, punishing bad deeds and rewarding good. Karma is about cause and effect: everything you do, think and say has a result. The Buddha said:

Wherever we go, wherever we remain
The results of our actions follow us.

All phenomena are interdependent, with our every act conditioning the next one. Nothing arises by itself. In this verse, the Buddha shows the importance of thoughts in creating our karma:

The thought manifests as the word;
The word manifests as the deed;
The deed develops into habit;
And habit hardens into character.
So watch the thought and its ways with care,
And let it spring from love
Born out of concern for all beings.

Your mother was always helping her friends. You see a mother in need, remember your own mother's example and help your friend. It was easy enough to do and made you feel good so you help your friend again. Soon you start helping more friends and before you know it you have the character of a helpful person with a helpful person's destiny ahead of you.

A relation makes a derogatory comment about your children. You feel overwhelmed by the injustice, the hypocrisy, of such a remark. Rather than let the unthoughtful comment pass, you bristle and rush to your children's defense, creating tension between you and your relation. This happens again the next time you meet and your anger snowballs. Over time you become caught in the habit of reacting to someone whose comments are not worthy of a response and each time you do this your character hardens a little more into one that is 'defensive' and 'easily offended'. This subtly affects the way people see you and treat you, as well as your own chances of finding calmness and happiness.

In both these examples, you have an experience which leads to a **thought** or **feeling** which you eventually **act** on. You repeat the **action** and establish a **pattern** which soon becomes a **habit**. Our habits form our **character** and our character determines our **destiny**. This is how karma works.

When it comes to karma, the intentions behind our actions are far more significant than our actions. Actions motivated by a sense of guilt or duty, are of far less karmic value than actions inspired by love and concern. Interestingly, the Buddha taught that thoughts of love and concern for others have the best effect on your karma.

My friend Lorraine was staying with friends one weekend and found herself feeling virtuous as she washed up after every meal. She told herself that she was creating good karma for herself, but knowing that the intentions behind an action are more important than the action, she probed for what her motives might be. To be considered a 'good guest', to avoid being seen as a burden, to give herself a clear conscience—these were her motives. She also hoped that her hosts would remember and help with the housework when they came to stay.

Lorraine felt humbled on finding that although her action appeared generous, her motives were anything but. As she continued washing up she started doing a loving kindness meditation to transform her intentions into love and compassion for her hosts. She dwelt on how tired her hosts might feel, how kind they had been to her and how grateful she felt for their friendship. She cultivated a genuine wish for them to be happy and free from suffering.

To change our destiny once we are caught up in our habits and automatic reactions takes great effort. Every time you act in a certain way you increase the chances of acting in that way again because you have started to condition yourself. Repeated actions become patterns that we usually aren't even aware of, patterns that create the way we live.

In my own struggle with restlessness, confined to my living-room and wishing I was elsewhere, I can watch my thoughts settle into well-worn patterns. I condition myself to become increasingly negative-minded as I think: 'I'm bored; if only we had more local friends with children; if only our local friends were more available; I wish Marek would come home; nappy number 20 for the day; I can't face another kids' book; I don't feel like going to the park; I wish I hadn't eaten all that cake mix; if only the children were older; I'm tired of all the repetitive housework; here I go again loading the dishwasher; not another request for juice!'

If I regularly surrendered to these thoughts—which could go on for hours if I let them—I'd start to shape my character into one that is focussed on the negative. The Buddha gave plenty of tips for dealing with negative thoughts, some of which I explore in the next chapter on anger. One surprisingly effective way for me to escape the vortex of self-pity has been to do some mindful yoga stretches, albeit with children clambering over the top of me. Focussing on my body and breathing deeply into each stretch, I create instant and surprising energy for starting afresh—suddenly I'm playing chasings, dusting off the pram or kicking a soccer ball. I find that yoga can haul you back into your body at those times your mind is prone to travelling. Interestingly, my next-door neighbour, who teaches yoga, often plays with her two children in what can appear a wild and crazy fashion. She seems to take delight in time with her children and agrees that being in touch with your body, and what it needs, brings energy and presence.

In understanding karma we realise our future is in our own hands. We don't have to be the person we've always been nor lead the life we've always led—we have choices, but first we need to be aware of the patterns we've developed. Every moment of our lives we are making choices that we have to live with for the rest of our lives. This leaves little room for blaming our parents, our circumstances or the system, for our dissatisfaction. Even with the worst of external circumstances we can choose our inner responses: will we be angry, forgiving, sad or compassionate? Our responses to events are far more significant than the events themselves.

An understanding of karma persuades us to focus our attention on the present moment, for this is the only time available to influence our karma. As the Buddha put it:

> *If you want to know what your future life will be like, look at your life right now.*

Keep asking yourself, 'How can I best use the present moment?' The Buddhist message is one of great optimism: by training our minds, we can create good karma and improve our chances for happiness in the future.

What we can do

- Take time to practise mindfulness around your children to help them grow up feeling noticed, heard and understood.
- Wake up to the abundance of special moments in the most ordinary of days.
- Cultivate the 'Beginner's Mind' which sees every moment with fresh eyes and responds to what the moment requires.
- Look deeply to learn who your children are rather than projecting your hopes, fears and expectations onto them.
- Use mindfulness to discover what you can learn from each situation—are you making unrealistic demands on life or are you accepting the inevitable imperfection?
- Observe the comings and goings of your own body sensations, emotions and thoughts to cultivate the self-awareness that helps you grow.
- Avoid creating grievances to fit your passing emotional states.
- Be aware of any tension building up throughout the day and consciously release it.
- Notice your surroundings.
- Remember that mindful living provides you with energy, calmness and the potential for insights.

- Realise that you have the power to choose your emotional responses—stressed and irritated or spacious and accepting.
- As you observe the details of the present moment, avoid rating them 'good' or 'bad', 'pleasant' or 'unpleasant'.
- Remember you can practise mindfulness no matter what you are doing.
- Whenever you find the time, even if it's one minute, meditate.
- Realise that the only moment you can work with is the present, so use it to set up good karma for your future.
- Expect and accept your failures to be mindful. Be patient with yourself.

CHAPTER 3

finding calm

THERE ARE DAYS WHEN my children seem like players in some divine plan to make me a nervous wreck. Interspersed with days when they're a joy to be around are the days when I can no longer cope with their ghastly music, the torturous repetitions of videos and the endless demands. On those days, children provide ideal training ground for developing calm—if you can master calm around demanding children, then you're a master indeed.

Too many mothers feel overstretched by the demands of a busy household or the juggle of work and kids. We've all experienced long days at home struggling with mind states such as boredom, restlessness, purposelessness or even despair. We tend to assume that any calmness of mind can occur only when all our chores are done and the children are asleep or in care. So, effectively, we would be very lucky if we had one hour a day to feel anything like relaxed. In Buddhism, however, we find teachings that help us to be calm regardless of what we're doing or who we're with. In this chapter we look at how best to deal with some of the mind states that visit us, in particular guilt.

In using Buddhism to deal with negative mind states, we progress slowly, with little steps. I've found that any mother who has practised Buddhist techniques will claim they have helped her to become more patient and calm in her parenting, yet the change occurs over a period of time rather than overnight. As with many aspects of spiritual progress, a step forward may be followed by two steps back—there's rarely a straight line of constant improvement. The incentive, though, is that in the long-run the overall improvement is plain to see. The day will come when you will know you have progressed and when it will be clear to you that you're responding to situations more calmly.

Every mother I meet seems to have some difficulty to grapple with, whether it's a lack of family support, tension with her partner, not enough time to herself, sleep deprivation or worry about her child. I've never met a mother who didn't deserve truckloads of compassion, so why should we make our own self the exception? Rather than feeling guilty or frustrated when we grapple with disturbing emotions, we need to treat ourselves with all the more compassion and patience for any suffering they cause us. It helps me to remind myself often that compassion for myself and my own difficulties and failings is the first step to living a compassionate life.

Dealing with negative mind states

Motherhood introduces us to mind states and extremes of emotion that can feel quite unfamiliar and disconcerting. In her book *Life After Birth, What Even Your Friends Won't Tell You About Motherhood,* Kate Figes writes:

> We revisit the raw emotions of our own childhood when we have a child. We feel intense love, undiluted hate and anger, as well as extreme anxiety and fear, and can swing from one extreme emotion to another.

She also points out the additional pressure to hide any anxiety we feel for our children's welfare so they can face the world with courage. Yet we need to cope not only with the emotions our children evoke but also those that arise as we adjust to the lifestyle of a mother. When we think back to our pre-mothering days of relative self-indulgence, for example, we may feel overwhelmed at how much we've sacrificed.

How can we manage all these complex emotions so we can achieve some peace of mind?

Nothing lasts

'Fed up.' 'Pushed too far.' 'At the end of my tether.' 'At wit's end.' 'At the brink.' 'Depressed.' These are the emotional depths we can sink to as mothers.

When I'm feeling at my lowest ebb emotionally, I notice my tendency to generalise the negativity: everything is dreadful, it always has been and it always will be and it's all my fault—and everybody else's too. It sounds almost comical when I'm in a lighter mood but at the time I believe these thoughts. With its emphasis on impermanence, Buddhism helps us at such times acknowledge that the mood will pass, that we won't feel like this for long and might even feel quite happy in a few hours' time; we can weather it for now and avoid assigning it any major significance.

The teaching of impermanence is a gift for our children too, even when they're quite young. We can use our understanding of impermanence to help them after they have experienced darker emotions—we can talk to them about how they felt, the way the feeling lasted for a few minutes and then changed into another emotion. From this they will learn that the dark places they stumble into have no lasting grip on them.

Identifying the lesson

My Buddhist friend Joanne has not been in Australia for long and is going through that tough first year that all migrants have to endure. Back in South Africa, she worked as a lawyer for female victims of violence. Recently I caught up with Joanne after what was for her a particularly taxing weekend. She lamented how challenging her life as a mother was, even compared to her demanding life as a lawyer in South Africa:

> I used to write books, defend the oppressed, go to Tai Chi and pottery classes. I've just spent all weekend in and out of hospital with sick children or holed up in my living room mopping their brows and thinking 'what has become of me?'. Although I've been a mother for over five years now, I'm still reeling from the culture shock.

As a consolation, Joanne reminded herself of that useful expression from Zen Buddhism, 'The whole world is medicine.' In any situation we can ask ourselves what we should be learning, or how our predicament could possibly be healing us. Buddhism helps Joanne to be philosophical about all the adjustments life is forcing on her. She later emailed me:

> I have to learn the lessons of humility which is why I find myself at this time, confined to domesticity, out of my networks, beyond a 'reputation' I had established, trying hard to find out who to be in this new country. Unnoticed, a non-earner, the epitome of everything I never wanted to be (at home, a full-time mom, dependent on a man), I find that there are many gifts in this space of quiet pausing between who I was and who I will become.

Motherhood does force us to reflect on our lives, on what's important to us and on how we want to live the rest of our lives. It also makes us question all our values and we find so many of our former opinions turned on their heads—especially when it comes to issues of raising children. When motherhood is tormenting us we can at least embrace it as the world's greatest Learning Experience, whether or not we agree with many Buddhists who believe that the lessons we fail to learn in this life will be the exact lessons we need to resolve in the next.

Hospitality

To help us survive the ebb and flow of all the emotional states that visit a mother, we assume an attitude of hospitality towards the emotions we receive throughout the day. We need to attend to each emotional 'visitor', pleasant or unpleasant; we don't avoid them or send them away. We accept and spend some time with each one without becoming too emotionally involved or taking any too seriously, keeping them all in perspective. We don't tell ourselves, 'I can't stand this one', for we can—we have survived this visitor in the past, so we will again. Nor do we travel into the future with nightmarish scenarios of where this visitor might take us, but rather stay with it in the present moment.

One Buddhist mother I know who finds this idea of hospitality helpful tries to greet her emotions as they arrive or as she realises their presence. Adopting similar vocal expression to that which she uses for visitors at her front door, she says, 'Oh! Anger. It's you.' or,

'Hello Boredom. You're here again.' and, 'Oh! Restlessness. It's your turn.' She says such mental greetings help her to take one step back and create some space between herself and the emotion. Seeing each emotion as a visitor is also a valuable reminder for her that it won't stay forever.

When we ignore these visitors or distract ourselves from the presence of disturbing states of mind, we lose touch with our feelings and our wisdom. We might seek to numb ourselves by indulging in alcohol, drugs, shopping, binge eating or blaming. Running away from our problems in this fashion empowers the negative mind states to do more damage than necessary—and we miss the opportunity to heal ourselves with awareness.

We may be scared of some of our mind states. Perhaps we harbour painful memories of times when we let them run out of control or times when we mistook them for who we were. Yet we don't have to act on what we find in our mind—in fact, our actions are likely to be wiser if they come from an awareness rather than a denial of our more obnoxious visitors.

Accepting the existence of feelings such as hatred, loneliness, confusion, anger, guilt and resentment, is the only way to transform them into more wholesome states. This is the path to wisdom: accepting life's unpleasantness, without fighting, fleeing or forcing it out of our awareness. We also remind ourselves that by fully experiencing our emotions, we deepen our understanding of others' pain and joy too.

Responding mindfully

To be mindful of our emotions, we need to stand back and watch them without condemning ourselves. We notice, without judgement, the thoughts that are fuelling the mind state as well as any body sensations and tensions. This mother who practises mindfulness explains:

> As a mother I struggle with feelings of frustration: there are always things I would like to be doing but can't because my children need so much attention. Buddhism helps me keep

> this frustration under control, not by suppressing it but by watching the effects of my feelings: how I talk to myself, the tight shoulders, the frown, the shallow breath. I try to watch the development of the emotion and the chattering of my mind. I start to breathe more consciously, I smile and release the muscle tension.

Just as the mindful monk described by the Buddha tells himself he is sitting, standing, lying down, etc., so we can label our inner experiences making acknowledgements such as 'feeling . . . feeling . . . feeling'. Whether during meditation or in daily life, this labelling is a way to remain an observer, to stay in the driver's seat rather than become a passenger driven by emotions running out of control. If we feel ourselves growing tense, we note slowly, 'tensing . . . tensing . . . tensing' and then perhaps, 'releasing . . . releasing . . . releasing' as we relax the tension. We can label an emotion that arises, repeating slowly, 'anger . . . anger . . . anger' or, 'guilt . . . guilt . . . guilt'. Without judging anything as good or bad, we watch the emotion arise, have being and pass away—as all emotions eventually do. No emotion need overpower us.

On seeing our mind state for what it is, we may experience a moment of clarity. Buddhist teaching has been summarised with the phrase 'stopping and realising' which, among other things, refers to the ability to be aware of a negative state of mind and to realise on a deep level that a clearer, more constructive mind is available. To understand that the negative mind state can only sabotage your efforts to improve a situation, is to instantly take on the more positive alternative. You 'awaken' to what the moment truly requires of you. Delusion turns into clear-sightedness.

Guilt

Some mothers say they barely live a moment without it. Worrying about whether we have given enough of our time and energy to our children is a source of pain for many working mothers and the younger the children the greater the worry. And mothers find many more reasons to suffer guilt. We might feel we've failed to be the perfect mother, permanently fulfilled by motherhood. We neglect other relationships we don't seem to have enough time for: those with our partners, family, friends and community. We torment ourselves with thoughts that whatever we are doing at the moment we should really be doing something else. When we do housework, for example, we feel we should really be reading books with our children and vice versa.

Guilt is a confusing emotion because although it clearly undermines our happiness, it's easy to tell ourselves that it's a worthy mind state. We can see guilt as a way of controlling ourselves. We even say to ourselves, 'I might be doing something wrong but at least I feel guilty—if I didn't feel guilty then I'd be a really terrible person.' In the same way we use guilt to ward off disapproval from others as we try to convince them that at least we feel really bad about our failure to be perfect.

We need to treat guilt in the same way that we treat any other visiting mind states. It requires our attention, not in the form of worrying and hand-wringing, but in the form of mindfulness. We need to be with our feelings of guilt, feel the effect of guilt on our body sensations. Importantly, we must identify the beliefs fuelling our guilty thoughts, as well as monitoring how much time we apportion to this mind state and how much of it is helpful.

If you need to solve a tricky dilemma, such as whether to use childcare, do so with a pen and paper and, if time allows, a mind calmed by meditation. When writing, you can be more conscious of your thoughts, so they are less likely to take over and torture you. Write out questions that allow you to explore your complex feelings. Do you have any irrational beliefs or expectations fuelling your guilt? Are you trying to appease a judgemental friend, relative or society? What hard evidence do you have to support your worrying? To make a decision, write lists of pros and cons and weigh the importance of the items in each list. By making the process conscious in this way, you can resist the tendency to stew.

I've always been an avid diary writer for exactly these reasons. Thrashing through my issues on paper is a way to tidy up a scattered mind, organise my thinking and brainstorm my options. I've been able to solve my problems consciously rather than reacting from anger, boredom, guilt or other unhelpful states. I have a pros and cons list for almost every major decision I've ever made and hundreds of pages where I've explored disturbing emotions. Although I rarely re-read them, I couldn't do without this tool for mindfulness.

In the same way, you can use meditation to resolve feelings of guilt or solve disturbing issues. Rather than our usual thinking approach, where we tie ourselves in knots and become stuck or obsessed, finding some stillness of mind in meditation allows us to bring spaciousness and perspective to our problems. Start by finding some stillness by concentrating on your breathing. Then bring a spirit of enquiry to your problem where you look at the facts objectively. You resist going on the journey of any compelling thoughts and emotions that arise, but rather notice all your reactions and how they contribute to the issue. Creating such space around your problem might lead you to be creative with your solution. New possibilities may suddenly enter your mind.

Embrace all things—equanimity

The word 'equanimity' is one that I only seem to hear in the context of Buddhism. It's a shame it's not more widely used because the concept is so inspiring and life-nourishing. It's the ability to perceive all aspects of our lives with acceptance and patience rather than our usual extreme reactions. Equanimity is the ability to keep calm whatever is happening. When something normally considered 'bad' happens, you can handle it—it doesn't derail you. Likewise, if something 'good' happens, you feel joy without feeling dependent on or attached to the event.

In *Teachings on Love*, the widely respected Vietnamese monk Thich Nhat Hanh offers these words to help us understand what equanimity is:

- inclusiveness
- even-mindedness
- non-attachment
- non-discrimination
- balance
- freedom from extremes
- letting go.

The Buddha taught that the greatest happiness comes from a peace unaffected by changing conditions. Therefore, an enlightened being embraces all that life presents, nothing can agitate or overexcite them. For the rest of us, any efforts to cultivate equanimity help us become calmer. To respond with equanimity doesn't mean we become indifferent to the course of our lives. We become more like the wise parents who can release their grown children into the world of adults. The wise parents still care about their children but can let go and accept their freedom. They have no need to control them, invade their new-found space or worry. They don't make demands. They aren't needy.

Accepting imperfection

My friend Joanne learned one important lesson from her experience of labour: if she was to cope with her new life she would have to surrender control. She had prepared for her labour meticulously—barely a book she hadn't read, scarcely a detail she hadn't planned—and was expecting a natural birth:

> I wanted midwives, candles, incense and pain.

As it turned out:

> After 34 brave hours of labour, I gratefully accepted when a male doctor offered to slice me open and relieve me of my ordeal.
>
> And from that moment, my life's mission of being my own boss, was terminated. Here I was, a warrior, a fighter, in whose path men trembled with fear, at the beck and call of a shrivelled little ET person who did not understand that I was a woman who ran with the wolves. Suddenly all that I had imagined I was, was fundamentally challenged by this new state. I had strived all my life for independence. Respect. Control. Now, I was a leaking, sagging, encumbered zombie.

With equanimity we accept 'what is' and stop trying to control the inevitable and the impermanent. Buddhism speaks of Eight Worldly Conditions: life is gain and loss, pleasure and pain, praise and blame, fame and disrepute. No matter how hard we try to attract or avoid any of these, we'll experience all of them in their turn. Each will come and go, just as every aspect of our lives is constantly changing. We never know what's round the corner and this can leave us ill at ease, yet to expect complete stability or control over events is unrealistic and ensures that we suffer more than necessary. Mother of two and Zen teacher Susan Murphy, offers these words of comfort to the perfectionists among us:

> It's important to notice the diabolically difficult nature of parenting and to not expect perfection. There is no perfection in the world and we don't have to be perfect. Instead we work with the life that is mysteriously ours with its own particular weave of love and pain. And we agree to be present to it, to accept the offer moment by moment, to develop unlimited friendliness for what is and who we are.

As mothers, we often find it hard to relax around our children, never knowing what the next moment will bring: a mess? a demand? a mood swing? danger? To be calmer we must learn to let go of some of our attachment to stability, control and order, and accept that our conditions constantly change. With equanimity we stop battling our way through life and begin to take it as it comes, to roll with the punches. We develop tolerance, defined here by Susan Murphy:

> It's because the love we feel for our children is so fierce that we are able, moment by moment, to lower our threshold of tolerance. Tolerance doesn't mean being relaxed and comfortable. It means accepting discomfort and finding ease in that accepting of discomfort.

We find tolerance through discovering the spaciousness of our minds and guarding against any tendency for our minds to become narrow, petty and small. If you add a spoonful of poison to a glass of water then a mouthful could be fatal. Add the same amount of poison to a vast lagoon, take a mouthful and you suffer no harm. An acquaintance makes an insensitive remark. With a small mind we overreact, perhaps stewing over the comment for days. With a spacious mind we can shrug it off—it's not important.

All those little things

Consider all the situations where we tend to 'lose it' and throw away our chance to experience peace in the all-important present moment. So often the incidents that undo us are of no lasting consequence and in losing it we ignore the other responses available to us. Imagine how different daily life could be if we could cultivate a spacious mind of equanimity. Your child spills some milk on the carpet: equanimity. Your son grizzles of an evening: equanimity. Your daughter acts sullenly. Your partner works late. Unpleasant noises, smells, sights: equanimity. Otherwise we allow so many details to disturb us that really needn't and our impatient reactions soon become a habit.

We forget that the innumerable irritations around us needn't control us. We might even slowly learn to welcome them as opportunities to practise patience. Thich Nhat Hanh, for example, advises us to smile at red traffic lights. Although at first such advice seemed bizarre, practising this helps me release tension and reach my destination in better form.

Fiona has two sons aged three and 14. Having practised Buddhism for three years, she comments on how it has affected life at home:

> I know I've become a somewhat 'milder' person, not losing my temper as quickly and, considering I have a teenager, I'm quite proud of myself. Another thing I've noticed, if an accident happens at home, a drink gets knocked over or the towel gets dropped in the bath water, it just doesn't matter, you clean up and get on with things.

Fiona's practice has clearly increased her potential to bring equanimity to the petty irritations of daily life.

But equanimity doesn't only apply to 'bad' events. When an event occurs that we label as 'good' we sometimes develop feelings of attachment that can undermine our calm. If we allow ourselves to depend on these pleasant events for our happiness, then we are attached. With equanimity, we can celebrate our child's dazzling result in the spelling test or swimming carnival without demanding repeat performances. We can appreciate our neighbour's offer to babysit or cook without feeling angry if they fail to follow through. We enjoy a few chocolate biscuits without needing to consume the packet in one sitting.

Developing equanimity

Those with equanimity know that each moment is of equal importance. Changing a nappy, wiping a nose, reading a story or waiting in a queue—all are opportunities for mindfulness, for growing wiser. Each moment is brilliantly new. It will not last, for it is in the process of changing into something else—this makes it precious. The truth about reality lies in each moment. The trick is to perceive it with complete acceptance, free of judgement, rating and demands—and of course to pay attention to it in the first place.

The Buddha said:

> *Do not pursue the past*
> *Do not lose yourself in the future.*
> *The past no longer is.*
> *The future has not yet come.*
> *Looking deeply at life as it is*
> *In the very here and now,*
> *The practitioner dwells*
> *In stability and freedom.*

We practise equanimity in meditation when we refrain from judging anything that happens. Our attention wanders: we don't chide ourselves but bring it back to the breath. We feel an itch: rather than rushing to relieve it we might spend some time exploring the sensation. We feel restless or bored: again we don't judge ourselves for feeling this way but sit with the feelings, watch them arise, exist and eventually fade away.

As the Buddha guided:

> *When seeing, just see. When hearing, just hear. When smelling an odour, just smell it. When tasting, just taste. When experiencing a tactile sensation, just experience it. When sensing a mental object, just sense it. Let things stop right there and insight will function automatically.*

Practising mindfulness helps us to be calm and peaceful, to keep all events in perspective.

It might seem that practising equanimity would lead us to suppress our emotions or try to control their intensity. But this is not the case. Equanimity comes automatically with the deepening of practice and with spiritual progress—we don't ignore or flee any mind states on the way. If anger or irritability knock at our door we watch them arise, exist and pass away without giving them any power. In this way we feel our emotions but respond calmly to them by refusing to let them entangle us.

A sense of the absurd and humorous

Once you have developed a degree of equanimity and spaciousness, you may find yourself laughing at incidents that used to enrage you.

A quick poo story (mothers are used to these).

One rainy Sunday when my first son was two, my husband was playing sport in a hall at the University of Sydney. Longing to read the newspaper in peace, I was driving my son Zac around the university buildings, hoping he'd fall asleep. After 15 minutes he was still awake and I watched my frustration rise. To calm myself, I was trying to focus on my breath and the sensations in my body, when Zac announced, 'I want to do poo.'

I had no idea where a toilet might be and it would have been dangerous to waste time looking. Parking under a 'No Stopping' sign, we clambered into the rain and Zac did his deed. While pulling his pants up I dropped my set of six keys directly into his poo. They sank in perfectly. Running to the car—to find I had no tissues—I saw a parking policeman in the distance, slowly making his way towards me. I had no choice but to hurriedly clean my keys with wet leaves as my son repeatedly asked: 'Mummy why did you drop the keys in the poo?'

The interesting thing about this debacle was that as I was cleaning the keys I was smiling. My situation was so pathetic that it amused me. My husband was enjoying himself in a warm, dry hall while I stood wet, my fingers covered in poo, with no hope of reading the paper. As mothers we all have similar stories of mini-disasters that have no lasting consequences but can push you to the brink if you let them. You can either work yourself into a frenzy of stress or you can laugh. The mind of equanimity helps us to laugh, to keep such events in perspective so we avoid becoming too emotionally caught up.

Buddhist teachers I've met have exhibited this readiness to laugh. They may be talking about something completely devoid of humour yet every few minutes they emit a quiet giggle. I have often wondered why they were laughing, only to conclude that they have developed an ability to see the absurd in daily life and take it lightly. One of my favourite sounds in the world is the laughter of His Holiness the Dalai Lama. If ever there was a contagious laugh, his is it.

Our 'Buddha Nature'

The keys to peace and calmness are within. An uplifting message of Buddhism is that everyone is a Buddha at their core, with a Buddha's love and wisdom—this is our true nature. We are already complete, whole and good, but we obscure this fact with our fears and desires. Our life's work is to realise, to bring into being, our true self—our 'Buddha Nature'.

In *Buddhism Plain and Simple, The Practice of Being Aware Right Now, Every Day*, the Zen Priest Steve Hagen explains our innate goodness plainly and simply:

> You are already enlightened. All you've got to do is stop blocking yourself and get serious about attending to what's going on. You are not lacking a thing. You only need to stop blocking or interpreting your vision.

He argues that every moment provides us with a chance to wake up to reality, which only exists in the present. To see clearly in each moment is to be at one with our Buddha Nature.

Our Buddha Nature is always accessible—in seeking it we are not chasing something outside ourselves but trying to uncover what is already there. Hagen reminds us of the Buddha's last words:

Look not for refuge to anyone beside yourself.

When our world is contracting, when we feel trapped and weighed down, we can remind ourselves of this higher purpose of realising our true nature and make time to aspire to be the best we can be. To find comfort we need only turn inwards. Seeking out my Buddha Nature has helped me nourish compassion for myself—just as my higher self loves and nurtures my children so it can love and nurture me. When in meditation I dwell on the existence of a Buddha within who loves me perfectly, I'm left feeling stronger and more self-sufficient, and this brings calmness.

So we don't need to travel the world, collect impressive experiences or achieve endless milestones in order to feel complete. What we seek is within us. The answer is to change *where* we look for it.

What we can do

- As you grapple with the coming and going of emotions, be compassionate with yourself.
- Remind yourself that no matter how intense your current emotional state, it will pass. Find opportunities to share this teaching with your children.
- Ask yourself what you could be learning from a difficult situation. Remember the whole world is medicine.
- See each new emotion as a visitor worthy of hospitality—not to be avoided or suppressed but accepted.
- Watch and label your emotions, either 'feeling . . . feeling . . . feeling' or more specifically, for example, 'restless . . . restless . . . restless'.
- If you are caught up in a destructive emotional state, create some space to 'stop and realise' or awaken to a more helpful alternative.
- If you are struggling with feelings of guilt, write or meditate so you can resolve your feelings consciously.
- Strive to accept imperfection and discomfort—fighting them only creates more strain.
- Whenever you can, choose a spacious response to petty irritations.
- Try to appreciate the preciousness of every moment.
- Realise that there is a perfect Buddha within you. Allow your own Buddha Nature or higher self to be your strength and comfort.

Chapter 4

dealing *with* anger

OUR PARTNER MAKES INSENSITIVE comments, works late, doesn't help, snores or eats too noisily. Our children disobey us, fight, nag or whine. Family life presents the potential to spend large chunks of time in a state of anger. Sometimes we experience a mild form of anger, mere irritation or annoyance. It makes us snap at our children or bicker with our partner. At other times our anger overwhelms us and our thoughts turn violent or vengeful. Outside our families too, it's easy to think of someone, if not a list of people, who make us feel hostile. And we even feel angry with strangers: driving around our cities makes vicious warriors out of the gentlest among us.

There's certainly no shortage of causes for a mother's anger. One such cause is the sheer volume of work that family life demands of us, its constancy and the resultant lack of opportunity to attend to our own needs. At the worst of times, even a shower feels like an enormous treat and for some mothers the working hours demanded by small children are utterly punishing. In the book *Of Woman Born*, Adrienne Rich expresses how she felt when she stole some precious time to write, only to be interrupted by her child.

> I would feel his wants at such a moment as fraudulent, as an attempt moreover to defraud me of living even for 15 minutes as myself. My anger would rise; I would feel the futility of any attempt to salvage myself, and also the inequality between us: my needs always balanced against those of a child, and always losing. I could love so much better, I told myself, after even a quarter-hour of selfishness, of peace, of detachment from my children.

In a similar frame of mind, Buddhist mother Joanne wrote this poem about suppressing anger and giving up her former life:

> *. . . she fights the shame*
> *Of a temper at small infractions*

By her children (thank god for them)
Never knew such temper simmered
Aching to be lost.
She sinks into memories and dreams
Folding corners of herself down
Like a neat napkin
Hiding the stains, the dirt
Of her most wonderous gypsy self
So that this life—this perfectly happy life—
Might proceed without incident
Without tragedy.
She who writes this song to herself
Sings now for the selves
That have no place to be sung.

Both these women, like so many of us, feel outraged at the level of self-sacrifice required of mothers.

In Buddhism anger—and in particular *acting out* angry feelings—is seen as the enemy. If managed skilfully, anger has potential to equip us with the inner resources required to protect an underdog or work for justice. Taking us to the heart of matters, anger provides an opportunity for wisdom as we explore and resolve it. Still, as the greatest enemy of loving kindness, anger more often has a destructive influence. The unsettling effect of anger on our peace of mind and on our capacity for compassion, makes it a formidable threat to our spiritual life. The Buddha said:

Killing anger removes suffering and brings peace and happiness.
Anger is the single enemy that all the wise ones agree to kill.

Some of us may feel we're not particularly angry by nature. But anger not only manifests as an emotional outburst or a hostile confrontation. Anger includes many behaviours, from sulking and withdrawing to behaving coldly and making snide comments.

For women, anger is less socially acceptable, which forces many of us to suppress it. Often we only find out how much anger we harbour by meditating—with mindfulness we become more aware of the emotions that writhe beneath the surface. In fact many meditators are amazed at how much anger they have been storing over the years.

The trouble with anger

In the first few weeks after Alex was born I was averaging about four hours of broken sleep a night. When Alex latched onto my breast it felt like a stapler, making me scream with pain several times a day. Full of joy over my new baby I was also reeling from the disruption to family life. I was an emotional yo-yo. One Saturday my husband dared to be in a somewhat negative mood for most of the day. I was incensed. If anyone was allowed to be in a bad mood it should have been me. It was his job to support and encourage me in my heroic efforts as a life-support unit. I weathered the day holding my tongue.

My husband has always described me as 'patient', so he was more than a little surprised when that night I marched into our bedroom, grabbed the bedside lamp, threw it at his face and broke it (the bedside lamp). That was not a very smart thing to do, for then my husband refused to talk to me. I sat in the baby's room wondering what my next move should be, when it occurred to me that I was supposed to be a non-harming Buddhist who refuses to act on anger. I returned to the bedroom, apologised and launched a quiet but stirring speech (I felt stirred anyway) about how during those difficult and testing weeks we needed to pull together and work as a unified team, et cetera, et cetera. We talked, the tension dissipated and all was well again. I'd love to say we then made passionate love into the night, but as parents of a newborn we were too tired to give it a thought.

Many mothers see anger as protection against being exploited—people might walk all over them if they didn't get angry. But we can still be firm with our children and assertive with others without giving in to anger. Anger in fact paves the way for future difficulties. For starters, it's not good for our karma: every time we act angrily we increase the chance we'll act angrily again, conditioning ourselves to become belligerent.

We may experience a sense of relief as we express anger, a glorious moment of self-righteousness as we assure ourselves: 'Well, I certainly showed them!' But the great irony of anger is in the way it does more damage to ourselves than to the objects of our anger, be they family members, friends, acquaintances or strangers. We may see anger as an inevitable response and give up our freedom to choose a more wholesome alternative. Unchecked, anger takes our energy, threatens our health and undermines our ability to make wise decisions. And holding a grudge poisons our peace of mind and leads us to justify our actions in ways that undermine any potential for self-awareness.

Closely related to hatred, anger can lead to a downward spiral of violence and destruction, as we see for many nations and religious groups: each new atrocity fuels more anger so the violence can never end. The Buddha said:

Hatred can never cease by hatred. Hatred can only cease by love. This is an eternal law.

In our relationships we see that angry actions from one party tend to induce angry, or at least defensive, actions in the other. The only way to stop the disintegration is to introduce more loving actions. As this mother found:

> For a few years my husband and I became stuck in a rut of anger. We seemed to have regular confrontations that didn't help either of us get what we wanted. If I attacked him, he would instantly defend himself without considering whether I had a good point to make and of course I'd do the same when he attacked me. Eventually we realised that our approach was

only polarising us and entrenching us both in our original viewpoints. And needless to say, the atmosphere of the house was far from pleasant. We knew that we'd have to find new ways to resolve our differences, particularly for the kids' sake. We began to focus on ridding our household of anger. We started discussing grievances more calmly and thoughtfully, even leaving the room if we felt the heat rising.

Taming anger

To help us deal with anger skilfully we can acknowledge the truths of impermanence and suffering. First we need to realise that although anger may consume us in the present moment it's still a transitory, impermanent state. To *act* on this transitory state would be damaging so we exercise restraint; we pause. We also remind ourselves of the first Noble Truth that suffering, imperfection and unsatisfactoriness are an inevitable part of life. Getting angry won't change this so why waste our emotional energy?

So what can we do when anger takes hold of us? It won't help to scold ourselves—to be angry with ourselves for feeling angry only adds fuel to the fire. Rather, we need to stare at our anger with determination, to be with it until it changes form or dissipates. We are careful not to indulge our anger or become absorbed by it. We see it as just another visitor without letting it toss us around emotionally. Yvonne Rand, mother and Zen priest interviewed by Vicki Mackenzie in *Why Buddhism?,* understands the Buddhist teachings of impermanence and watching our anger:

> . . . when my kids were young, if I got frightened I would express it as anger, and then I would feel just terrible. One of the very significant consequences of meditation for me was to learn how to deal with that strong negative emotion—neither suppressing nor expressing it. I saw there was a third option which was to be able to be present with it, not denying it, nor

> stuffing it down, nor letting it out. If you get angry and upset you can pay attention to what you are feeling in your body, in your stomach, the tightness in your throat, whether your chest feels constricted—you can even acknowledge that there is a lot of anger coming up. It's one thing to describe and acknowledge it and another to act it out. I soon realised that whatever emotion was coming up would dissipate extremely quickly. With my children it was very useful.

The Tibetan teacher Geshe Kelsang Gyatso—in *Transform Your Life*, one of his many books—writes that anger has three components:

1. We perceive an *object that we find unpleasant.*
2. We *exaggerate* the perceived harm.
3. We develop a *wish to harm.*

Recently I went on a family retreat with my two sons for a couple of nights. 'Retreatants' were all warned to keep the noise down around the dormitories at night. It was around 9.30 p.m. and my son Zac was very tired after a day full of adventure. With very little reason he started moaning loudly—as three year olds do when they're tired—right outside the dormitories. Panic-stricken, I tried in vain to clamp his howling mouth shut as I imagined every child waking and every parent cursing. Another retreatant came to my aid and carried baby Alex as I grabbed Zac and hauled him to our room in a rage.

I was extremely angry as Zac continued to bellow, telling the other retreatant that I was hurting him. Surrounded by dormitories I couldn't even shout at him. Holding his arms a little too tightly, all I could do was whisper, through clenched teeth, threats of a sudden end to our holiday. The other retreatant was watching me and I felt ashamed of myself, my image as a calm, loving Buddhist mother blown. She put Zac to bed as I breast-fed Alex who had also started to cry. Zac fell asleep almost as soon as she left the room and I emitted a sigh of exasperation. The next morning I walked into the breakfast room. Fifteen faces looked at me and I just knew they'd heard all about my family's little scene. I was wrong—most of the children had been sleeping deeply and the adults had been off meditating in the shrine.

All three components of anger are illustrated in this episode. I *perceived an object that I found unpleasant*: Zac, who was shouting and possibly waking people up. I *exaggerated the harm*: everybody would wake up and be angry with me, talk about me and stare knowingly at me at breakfast. I *wished to harm* my son: I wanted to scare him with the idea of ending the holiday; I wished I could shout at him and make him fear and obey me. And perhaps a darker part of me wanted to smother him—temporarily . . . I don't remember now.

Anger leads to a harming mind which, if we want to make spiritual progress, we must abandon. There are two stages to this abandonment: first we recognise the negative force of the anger and see it as the enemy; then we try to look within ourselves to understand the causes and eliminate them. Anger tends to focus our mind on external conditions, making it hard to turn inwards to seek the causes of the problem and this is why blaming and frantic self-justification are our natural responses to anger. But when we turn inwards, we discover our views of what is 'good' and what is 'bad'—we find attachment and aversion.

Turning inwards after my incident on retreat, I discovered the terror I've always felt at the prospect of making others angry with me, even if they are being unfair. I automatically experience strong and exaggerated aversion to disappointing or displeasing others. I seem to need a blemish-free report card from everybody. In the service of this aversion, I expected my three year old to angelically keep quiet and be considerate of others when he was still at the egocentric stage in his development. Looking deeper still, I meet my inner critic who tells me that if I disturb others I'm a less worthwhile, less valuable person. Unless I'm pleasing everybody all the time I'm a failure. How ridiculous our irrational beliefs can appear when we put words to them; yet we allow them to shape our whole lives. In retrospect I realise I could have seen the humour in the situation rather than fuelling Zac's outburst. At the very least I needn't have overreacted to such an extent.

Geshe Kelsang Gyatso advises us to use meditation to generate a strong determination to abandon the mind of anger. We repeat to ourselves, 'I won't give in to anger' or 'I will abandon the mind of anger'. Such a preventative measure prepares our minds—programs us, if you like—for events that might trigger our anger. We work on developing a mind of patient acceptance which allows us to stop insisting that life be other than it is.

Life will always present irritations and suffering. Only with a patient mind, that accepts whatever occurs, can we experience lasting happiness. As long as our happiness is conditional on external circumstances we won't know peace. With spiritual progress we become more patient and accepting of all circumstances. We develop equanimity. This doesn't mean we become passive or uncaring, but that a calm wisdom rather than emotional extremes informs our actions.

Dealing with the aftermath

And what about those times when it's too late: you've snapped and acted on your anger? Betsy has been practising Buddhism for over 12 years and gives classes in Buddhism in schools. Mother to a seven-year-old boy, Sam, she believes in making her practice transparent to him and, since he was three, has been sharing some of the details of her practice with him. Laughing, she admits that her son often gives her advice—he now has a very clear understanding that when she loses her temper it's usually not about him, it's a difficulty in her own psychological world.

As Betsy points out, we want our children to be able to apologise when they are in the wrong, so we need to model such behaviour to them. When she loses her temper she tries to take responsibility and admit to him that she was at fault. Betsy and Sam discuss incidents together, noting a) that her response was not helpful, and b) the need for an alternative approach. Then they discuss different ways to deal with such incidents. During these discussions she emphasises the teaching of karma, that every action has a consequence—when you said *x*, I felt *y* and when you did *a* then *b* happened.

Betsy has even come up with a 'Harsh Language Chart' as a way for both her and Sam to take responsibility. If either of them use harsh language and agree after some discussion that this is the case, a cross is put against the offender's name and at the end of the week, the one with the least crosses gets a treat. Betsy admits that she never gets the treat but that the chart has led to some very constructive discussions, for example, about the difference between firm, assertive language and inappropriate, aggressive language.

Many Buddhist mothers I've spoken to make a point of apologising to their children if they have lost their temper. Apologising, they say, is an effective way of 'letting go' of their anger, of humbling themselves. As this mother said:

> It's like giving some power over to your children rather than hoarding it all to yourself. Especially if you ask them to forgive you. So many parents think they have to appear perfect to their children but I think you're doing them a greater favour if you teach them ways to cope with being imperfect—as we all are. If you can tell them, from time to time, 'I made a mistake', you might find them willing to say the same back to you some day. Then they have learned to take responsibility for their behaviour.
>
> I also think we should warn our children if we're in a bad mood or finding it hard to cope. Sharing our state of mind with them saves them from taking our behaviour personally. Children need to know that our bad moods aren't necessarily their fault.

As for dealing with aggressive drivers, moody bosses and other stressed individuals who raise our ire, we can take inspiration from the Tibetans. The Dalai Lama and others speak of the way many Tibetans survived torture, without the usual psychological damage experienced by victims of trauma. The more spiritually advanced even felt compassion for their torturers, knowing their behaviour could only arise from deeply troubled minds. Realising the law of karma they knew the torturers would suffer greatly with such impure and deluded minds. As Westerners, we struggle to understand such a response but it's definitely an inspiring lesson we can apply to our own problems. We can tell ourselves it isn't always our job to punish offensive behaviour as the law of karma sees to this—we can even challenge ourselves to feel compassion for those creating bad karma for themselves.

As encouragement for us to abandon the mind of anger and all angry actions the Buddha said this:

The one who offends another
after being offended by him,
harms himself and harms the other.
When you feel hurt
but do not hurt the other,
you are truly victorious.
Your practice and your victory benefit both of you.
When you understand the roots of anger in yourself
and in the other,
your mind will enjoy true peace, joy and lightness.
You become the doctor who heals himself and heals the other.
If you don't understand,
you will think not getting angry to be the act of a fool.

Forgiveness

We can hit a stage in certain relationships where the only way to get on with our lives is to declare an amnesty, to forgive. If we continue to harbour resentments, living our days in anger for past hurts, our mind becomes too small for any joy in life. Although forgiveness can seem like an irrational response to insensitive behaviour, once we can forgive we let go of painful feelings and memories that cause us to suffer. It's an act of compassion we can feel proud of, an opportunity to revel in our spiritual progress. In some cases it's the ultimate act of love and compassion.

Admittedly, it's often unrealistic to replace the intensity of anger with forgiveness too soon after a hurtful episode. We can't forgive simply because we 'should'; we can't force it until we're ready—and this might take work. Such work might take the form of communication using skilful speech and mindful listening (see Chapter 7). Or it could be through loving kindness meditation that we plant the seeds of our intentions to eventually forgive (see Chapter 9).

Sometimes forgiveness can only be a long-term goal worked at over many years. We may need to wait for it to arrive and as we do we watch our emotions around a past event subtly transform. Rage may become a milder, less debilitating resignation. We may need to suffer agony on the road to forgiveness, but to relieve ourselves of the burden of a grudge, the effort is worth it.

Forgiveness can be a sensible acknowledgement that we all battle with delusion, confusion and imperfection. It may help to remember the times that we have caused harm to others, acted selfishly and required forgiveness. Or we might find we need to face up to our own responsibility in a conflict—were all our intentions, actions and utterances wholesome?

Be mindful of the effect that holding forgiveness back has on your body. Where do you store the tension? How does it affect your mind state? Understand the effect that a grudge has on you and on your karma. Imagine the ways in which your life would feel different if you were free of this grudge.

Taming unskilful thoughts

When we observe ourselves experiencing a state of anger, we notice that our thoughts are the fuel: 'I shouldn't have to put up with this!', 'This is utterly unbearable!', 'He has no respect for me whatsoever!', 'How dare she walk all over me like that!' So many of our problems begin with our thoughts. When we discussed karma, I quoted the Buddha's words about how thoughts shape our character, that we must therefore take care of them and ensure they are loving (see p. 34).

For us to have any hope of taming our tendency to anger we need to work with our thoughts. The first part of the task is to notice them rather than go for a ride with them. They can feel so powerful and compelling, and take us so far from the present moment, that we really need to 'stop and realise', or 'remember to remember' to pay attention. We then need to identify thoughts that are unskilful, unhelpful and keep us from being happy and calm.

In the Buddha's Discourse on the Forms of Thought he gave us five options for dealing with disturbing thoughts. In brief, he advised us to:

1. Dwell on the positive.
2. Consider the results of our thoughts.
3. Distract ourselves.
4. Consider the alternatives.
5. Use our willpower.

None of these are particularly ground-breaking. We hear this kind of advice all the time because it's what has worked through the ages. What I find helpful, though, is that the Buddha presents this advice as five *options* for us to choose from. He doesn't say, for example, whenever you have disturbing thoughts just dwell on the positive. Nor does he say, avoid disturbing thoughts using pure willpower. As we know, there is not one of these options that will be attractive to us in all cases. We can use our judgement and select the most useful option, or a combination of options, for the particular moment in which we find ourselves.

Dwell on the positive

The first option the Buddha suggested is:

> *If some unskilled thoughts associated with desire, aversion or confusion arise and disturb the mind, you should attend instead to another characteristic which is associated with what is skilled . . . It is like a skilled carpenter who can knock out a large peg with a small peg.*

Short of sleep or energy or both, mothers could end up walking around feeling angry with quite a list of people: our children, other people's children and plenty of Adults Who Should Know Better. For each person, we can remind ourselves of their qualities and any of their acts of kindness—just as we hope others will do for us when we have inspired their ire. I try to make a mental note when I notice any friends or relations acting generously and kindly. Then I can remind myself of such acts if I ever start to cast these characters in a negative light. This mother does the same for her partner:

> Consumed with anger, there are days when I dramatically declare to myself that my marriage is over and there's no way we could possibly make it to the finish line together. When I can collect myself off the rollercoaster that my thoughts are taking me on, I can remind myself of my husband's numerous good qualities and of the times when I felt grateful for his generosity or thoughtfulness.

We can also practise giving people the benefit of the doubt to cut off the negative thoughts before they start rolling by realising, for example, that a comment wasn't necessarily directed at us; people's lateness is not about us but their time management problem; our child's appalling behaviour is not a personal attack but a reaction to their change in routine.

Consider the results

The second option the Buddha suggested is:

> *Scrutinise the peril of these unskilled thoughts by thinking: 'these are unskilled thoughts, these are thoughts that have errors, indeed these are thoughts that are of painful results'.*

Remind yourself of the great irony of anger—it does so much more harm to you than it does to the perpetrators. Consider your own karma. Every time you choose a response of anger you condition yourself to respond in this way again. How will we ever know peace of mind if we condition ourselves to be angry people?

Personally, I have very painful regrets about times when I've handled difficulties with anger. Allowing tension to build over many years before exploding, not only did I make a fool of myself, but I did irreparable harm to my relationships. I've learned that it's so important to handle tension with care and restraint, to avoid acting on my anger and harming others.

So we need to ask ourselves: where are these thoughts taking me? Will I erupt like a volcano if I continue to think this way? When my second child, Alex, arrived and my mothering load increased, I felt a dramatic shortening of my fuse with my eldest. I was alarmed at this new capacity to lose my temper and even feel violent. Rather than blame a three year old for some of the uglier domestic scenes, I had to acknowledge the damage done by my own angry contribution. What sort of mother did I want to grow into? What kind of relationship did I want with my children? Did I want to add to my children's suffering? For my own sake too, I had to bring my newfound temper under control or my mental health might have suffered.

Distract yourself

The third option the Buddha suggested is:

> *Bring about forgetfulness and lack of attention to those thoughts . . . it is like a man who, not wanting to see the material shapes that come within his range of vision, would close his eyes or look another way.*

Buddhist teachings often speak of our tendency to give 'inappropriate attention' to minor events and work ourselves into a state of anger. At times, we become obsessive and repetitive in our thinking, revisiting past events and stewing over them. We need to be mindful, catch ourselves paying inappropriate attention and refuse to continue. Often, if we can abandon inappropriate attention, we can abandon anger. This requires a change in our focus. Mindfulness of the breath helps to relax us and stop the flow of inappropriate attention. In tense situations, breathing deeply is calming and grounding.

In our pre-motherhood days, distracting ourselves was often the perfect antidote to destructive thoughts. We could usually find some time in our day to grab a novel or skip off to the cinema. Not so these days: our children's needs are too immediate and we have to stay in the thick of it. Still, when our thinking is counterproductive, obsessive or unhelpful, we can distract ourselves by thinking along different lines.

I once found planning a dinner party a helpful antidote to a troubled mind. Bringing a Buddhist slant to the affair, I tried to prepare it out of love and a genuine desire to give my guests a wonderful experience. All week my mind space was taken up with planning the dishes and the details. The night itself now makes a very pleasant memory. Sometimes an effective distraction is to move your family unit outdoors. Or you can call a friend or seek some adult company. Do a crossword. Read a snippet of a magazine. Write a poem. Look for an inspiring recipe. Sort your photos.

As with the other options, this option of distracting ourselves is not the best answer for every situation. It's not appropriate when, for example, we need to address our feelings and resolve them.

Consider the alternatives

The fourth option the Buddha suggested is:

> *Even as it might occur to a man who is walking quickly: 'Now, why do I walk quickly? Suppose I were to walk slowly?' It might occur to him as he was walking slowly: 'Now, why do I walk slowly? . . . Suppose I were to lie down? . . . This man having abandoned the hardest posture, might take to the easiest posture.*

In a spirit of enquiry, question your thinking: why am I thinking in this way? What led me to think in this way. And then: is there an easier way to think? A way that would make my life flow more smoothly? We don't need to be tied down into one stifling version of our reality. Thoughts come and go and often have very little to do with *what is*. We don't need to empower them by believing them. This is one of the most common discoveries made by those who try mindfulness meditation: my thoughts are just thoughts, they are not me and they are not reality.

As the Buddha constantly reminded us, our mind creates our reality: what we tell ourselves is more powerful than the situation itself. It's up to us to decide how important we choose to make a disturbing event. When we feel irritated or angry we need to admit that we have chosen to perceive this disturbance and judge it as bad. Is there another way to interpret this situation? Do we need to take it so personally? Is this situation really worth such an emotional investment? Is anger the inevitable response? Through questioning, a more wholesome state might dawn on us.

One mother describes the split second where she switches her automatic response to her toddler:

I'm feeling crabby and I might be about to tell my daughter off for the twentieth time. But instead of 'Don't touch that!', I find myself saying, 'How about a tickle?' and we roll around on the floor enjoying a completely different moment to what might have been. It wasn't what I felt like saying but very soon my spirit caught up with my words.

Use your willpower

The fifth option the Buddha suggested is:

> *By the mind subdue, restrain and dominate the mind . . . It is like a strong man who, having taken hold of a weaker man by the head or the shoulders, might subdue, restrain and dominate him.*

If we are really determined to train our minds into a healthier state and if we make this a serious goal then we might have some success combatting unskilful thoughts through the force of our will. We might only need to be gentle but firm with ourselves, saying: 'Let go' or, 'Enough'. As Geshe Kelsang Gyatso suggests, we can use meditation time to generate a strong determination to abandon the mind of anger. It may be a matter of asking ourselves, 'How important are healthy relationships to me?' as well as, 'How important is my spiritual progress?'

What we can do

- Remember angry thoughts and words are bad for your karma.
- Remember anger is just a passing state so don't empower it.
- Acknowledge and be present with your anger without indulging it—watch its effect on your body, how it changes form and finally dissipates.
- Look inward for the causes of anger so that you can eliminate them.
- Use meditation to generate a strong determination to abandon the mind of anger.
- Share some of your struggles with your children so they too can learn from your mistakes—there's no need to teach them that you're perfect.
- Apologise to your children when you're in the wrong.
- Inform your children if you are in a bad mood so they don't take it personally.
- Consider forgiving those you are angry with—if only for your own sake.
- Consider the Buddha's five options for dealing with unwholesome thoughts:
  1. Dwell on the positive.
  2. Consider the results of your thoughts.
  3. Distract yourself.
  4. Consider the alternatives.
  5. Use your willpower.

Chapter 5

worrying *about* our children

MY LATE GRANDMOTHER WAS a worrier. She was many other things too, including a self-sacrificing family asset. Ever-present throughout my childhood, she was constantly babysitting my two sisters and me, telling us stories, watching our 'performances', listening to our childish ramblings. When not lavishing us with attention she was busily scrubbing any corner of the house with even a hint of grime. She lived to serve us, shunning the company of anyone who wasn't 'family'. A phonecall to Grandma could never be less than half an hour and not once in family history did she hang up first.

Less admiring relatives would say that, as the self-appointed family worrier, Grandma wasn't happy unless she was worried sick. She turned worrying into such an art form that we all agreed never to tell her any news that could trigger her imagination—and that seemed to restrict communication drastically. Her two children, my mother and uncle, avoided telling her when they were travelling overseas, going into hospital or facing even the slightest of challenges. Grandma was noble and loving, but sadly, as a compulsive worrier she missed out on large slices of our lives. She could never be a confidante, counsellor or listener when her loved ones were in distress.

It's a common story: daughters and sons bottle up their problems because they 'don't want to worry Mum'. Yet as mothers how can we help our children if they won't confide in us? How can we be their allies as they face problems like bullying, drugs, depression, or even thoughts of suicide? To help our children face these challenges we need to be, in their eyes, strong, resourceful and wise. And we must be heroic and hide the extremes of any anxiety we feel over their well-being.

My own mother was a skilled confidante. My sisters and I never hesitated to share our concerns with her and it never crossed our childish minds that we might be burdening her. One of my most poignant memories is when, in my early twenties, I was going through a painful phase and felt trapped and despondent. I spoke about my situation with my mother, then began to drive home. Realising I'd forgotten something, I returned to find her with a tear-stained face. She denied anything was wrong. Driving home again I felt deep gratitude. I realised that my mother had always presented a strong image in the face of our difficulties but perhaps she was more like Grandma than we'd thought: it was painful for her to see her children suffer.

Up to a point, worry can be useful for forcing us to plan, sift options or take action. Yet we tend to worry way past this point even though we know it won't help. If we give into this tendency, we can spend the rest of our lives worrying and never know peace. There seems to be two types of worrying: the first type is unnecessary or based on imaginary scenarios. As Mark Twain expressed it, 'My life has been filled with terrible misfortunes . . . most of which never happened.' Then there's worry that is well-founded or justifiable, such as when our children are genuinely suffering.

The costs of worrying

The toll of worry is both physical and mental. The medical profession tells us that constant worry dries up blood, weakens our body functions and leads to high blood pressure, heart problems, stomach ulcers and breathing difficulties. And we don't need a doctor to tell us that worry ruins our hopes of restful sleep, adequate energy levels and peace of mind. With a worry-prone mind, we may find ourselves avoiding certain situations and so limiting our potential and opportunities, along with those of our children.

Worry creates a troubled mind which undermines our effectiveness: we lose the ability to think clearly just as we lose perspective and the potential for a cool, calm response. As Adrienne Howley, a Buddhist nun and mother of two sons, writes in *The Naked Buddha*: 'If we are mentally busy clinging and craving, worrying about what we call security, our reactions will not be skilful and the outcome not what we had hoped for.' She argues we need to use mindful investigation and analysis in order to see things the way they really are and find solutions to our problems.

And as happened with my Grandma, the more you develop the habit of needless worrying, the harder it is to stop. It became her karma, her character, her destiny, to worry. Each time she worried she reinforced the habit, until it felt like a natural, inevitable mind state. Worrying is one of the most habit-forming behaviours we can engage in, forcing our minds to inhabit an imaginary and joyless future world. It leaves no room for awareness of the present moment.

One Buddhist mother, Sue, has suffered gravely from some of these costs of worry. She has watched, with a growing ache in her stomach, as her daughter has developed the same facial imperfections which made her suffer while growing up. Sue always perceived her face as a collection of undersized and oversized features and sadly, so did the more cruel characters in the school playground.

> I can't believe I have to relive some of the worst memories of my life through my poor daughter. That she could suffer even a fraction of my anguish breaks my heart and can at times make me feel quite depressed. I rarely talk openly about my anxiety because I feel I would be betraying her in some way. People might laugh, tell somebody or pity my daughter. So this is something I have to cope with alone. Sometimes I find myself looking at her and although I find her so beautiful I feel so full of sadness—my thoughts can end up depressing my mood and ruining my day. Then there are the days when I catch other children commenting on her appearance and it feels like a strong punch to my stomach. She's not taking it badly yet but I won't be able to protect her in the future.

Sue realised that her worrying could snowball into such a heavy weight that it could destroy any chance of peace for her mind. She could see her potential destiny as a tortured soul and tried to change her karma.

I knew I had to start managing my thoughts which were running out of control. One day I sat and meditated until I had reached a space of calmness. I then rose, sat at my desk and wrote and wrote. I wrote down all the feelings that my own sense of physical unattractiveness had evoked as I was growing up: isolation, humiliation, a sense of missing out, of not being respected. It helped to put words to these mixed up feelings: now they had been captured.

I then teased out and named all my fears around the issue of my daughter's appearance and tried to come up with a collection of more helpful thoughts or counter arguments. Perhaps my daughter would not be as sensitive and self-conscious as I was—suffering less deeply or in a different way. I was definitely quite a melancholy child prone to dwelling on my problems. Besides, her experiences will be different from mine or any scenario I could imagine. It's all a mystery so why waste my time guessing the horrors that could befall her.

She might have powerful redeeming features like a terrific sense of humour that helps her cope with any physical flaws and become one of those likeable types who 'don't take themselves too seriously'. I can help her to focus on other talents and abilities for her source of self-confidence. I can concentrate on creating a loving home and community around her which can soften the impact of any blows. Besides, a positive home environment would have to be the most important contributor to a child's happiness.

I can remind myself of others with similar physical imperfections who are leading relatively happy, successful lives. I could even seek out such people so that the role models are there to inspire her. Like me, these people have developed other aspects of their characters than their appearance and they tend to have some emotional depth.

The suffering she's likely to face might help her to grow

> into a mature, highly evolved person. She might learn important lessons like compassion for others. Maybe we have these physical characteristics for a reason and we both need to learn something from them. And my experience, if I manage myself wisely, could be of benefit to her. It could make us closer.
>
> Anyway, it helps me to come back to this list when my worries start to fester again. I can't say I've overcome my fears yet but having a list of counter-arguments helps me see more clearly. I don't get so engrossed in my ideas of a bleak future, so caught up in my own aversion. This is important because I know I can only help her if I'm calm and together.

How many of us wouldn't benefit from a thorough investigation into an issue that worries us? Whether on paper or in a formal meditation sitting, we all have the potential to confront our worries and even, to varying degrees, resolve them.

Accepting some suffering

With technological advances, we live in an age of quick-fixes, instant solutions and labour-saving devices. With the help of millions of advertisements, we are lulled into the false belief that we don't need to put up with any discomfort, anything 'negative', so we fight and resist discomfort, refusing to put up with it. We forget the first Noble Truth that there is suffering, that life is inherently unsatisfactory.

Throughout history, most women have lived in constant domestic drudgery, their children often fell seriously ill or died, their husbands owned them as property and marriage breakdown could push them into domestic labour or prostitution. Most women held no status in society, and found little compassion for their plight. To these women, suffering and unsatisfactoriness would have been such an integral part of life it would not have been questioned—and a large proportion of women around the world still live in such conditions. Compared to these women we are spoilt, with our 1.8 children, our modern comforts and our relative freedom.

Even still, our higher standard of living can't spare us from suffering and imperfection, regardless of what modern technology and advertisements promise. Modern women only experience new ways to suffer, as do modern men, for this is the nature of existence. What makes modern suffering especially painful is our belief that we needn't suffer, that we can't tolerate any discomfort and must stamp it out at any cost. We demand that life be other than it is, become attached to our vision of what should be, and feel intensely frustrated when our expectations are dashed.

Yet what we fear and worry about is not so much a situation as the emotions it triggers in us. We worry about how a dreaded event will make us feel or about how much more worrying might be ahead of us. It's not the suffering, the unsatisfactoriness, that hurts so much as our aversion to it, the emotional struggle against the suffering. Instead of trying to control external details it might be worth investing more effort in examining our emotional reactions. This could be a far more effective way to diminish our potential to suffer. In the words of Adrienne Howley: 'The mind free of worry . . . knows that it is not what happens to us that is of prime importance but how we react to it.' When we can't remove from our lives what we fear, instead of worrying it is better to practise patience, acceptance and equanimity. To continue struggling against the inevitable only fuels our suffering and unhappiness.

Dealing with worry

Contrary to what we usually assume, our worries don't afflict us from 'out there', but exist in our minds. If we can gain some control over our minds then we can influence the quality of our experiences. The Buddha said this in many ways, such as:

We are what we think. All that we are arises with our thoughts. With our thoughts we make the world.

Your worst enemy cannot harm you as much as your own mind, unguarded. But once mastered, no one can help you as much.

Mind is the forerunner of all states. Mind is chief; mind-made are those states.

The person who suffers most in this world is the person who has many wrong perceptions . . . And many of our perceptions are erroneous.

In meditation and mindful living we develop the ability to watch our thoughts and follow the scary stories we invent. We notice any snowballing, where each new thought is slightly more dramatic than the last. We notice distortions and exaggerations of reality to the extent that we can relate to the scene in the movie *Parenthood* where Steve Martin, tortured by his parenting difficulties, drifts into a fantasy in which his young son is the gunman in a playground massacre.

As we saw in the case of anger, worrying can be the product of inappropriate attention—we choose to perceive only the narrowest slice of reality, exaggerate it and dwell on it, effectively allowing our perceptions to imprison us. The well-known Vietnamese monk, Thich Nhat Hanh, explained in *Teachings on Love* the need to be firm with your own mind when you catch yourself worrying: 'If we are mindful, we will . . . release inappropriate attention, noting, "I am aware that this inappropriate attention will not benefit me or those I care about".'

What are you clinging to?

We need to uncover any irrational beliefs that lead to worry. Everything we worry about comes from some kind of mismatch between our beliefs and our experiences. We believe things should be a certain way and they aren't. So it makes sense to constantly tease out the beliefs that give rise to all our worries. This mother has realised the price of holding opinions too tightly:

> With my religious upbringing I came to see the world in terms of unhelpful dualities: good and bad, heaven and hell, happy and sad, safe and dangerous. The job for me now is to transcend this dualistic thinking. Seeing the world in a rigid black and white, either/or way has only created tension and anxiety for me. I need to let go of my tightly held opinions about what's good and bad. My focus now is on striving for equanimity and stability.

Perhaps you believe it would be terrible for your children to suffer, that they should always be happy. On identifying such a belief you ask yourself how rational it is and decide that it's not very rational at all. Children need to learn from disappointments and suffering just as we do. You might decide that you could be more philosophical or accepting when it comes to your children suffering. Psychologists claim that childhood difficulties can be excellent preparation for adulthood and that a lack of difficulty in childhood could well produce an adult who flounders. Protected from life's blows children never learn to be wise, compassionate or sensitive.

Professor Martin Seligman, one of the most influential psychologists in the United States, appeared in a documentary called *Myths of Childhood* with a strong point to make:

> I think parental and educative efforts to have our children feel good all the time simply weaken our children. They deprive our children of being skilled at coping with the failures and rejections that life inevitably brings us. Movements which say our children should feel good all the time have deprived our children of the skills of coping with depression, have set our

> children up for adult bad feelings just as surely as if we had physically thwarted them, humiliated them at every step of their development.

The Buddha's father learned the hard way that despite his wealth and position as a King, he could not protect his son, Siddhartha, from the world. Although he tried to create the perfect childhood where his son would want for nothing, his son insisted on his freedom to see the world as it was. Like Siddhartha and every human ever to exist, our children must suffer. The more we resist this and insist against it, the more it will hurt us. Although we still care deeply for our children and do our best to help them cope with suffering, we need to protect our minds from the ravages of ceaseless, aimless worry.

If we can observe our worrying we can uncover the demands we make on life, or in Buddhist terms, areas of attachment which cause suffering and anxiety. The more demands we have, the more our potential to worry. Could we convert our stubborn demands into something milder, say, 'preferences'? Perhaps we could shift from, 'My child *must* excel academically', to 'It would be nice if my child could excel academically but it won't kill us if they can't'. Clearly, the second attitude is far more conducive to peace in the minds of all family members.

I have a wise friend, Anna, whose nine-year-old son, as a toddler, was slower than his peers with his speech development. Today she says he's not very academic and he's quite clumsy on the sports field. At the same time, he delights in fixing, tinkering and creating with his hands and is endlessly resourceful. Anna marvels that certain family members have worried and fretted over her son's not being an 'all-rounder', but Anna doesn't demand that her child be perfect nor that he keep pace with his classmates. Of course, she does everything she can to help him and arrange tutoring, but she accepts and loves him for who he is and refuses to worry about what she can't change. She is concerned, but not worried. She shows she cares without showing impatience which might hurt her son, a cheerful boy who's clearly enjoying his life.

In some cases, the demands we harbour for our children show not love but attachment. If we insist that our children make us proud or enhance our self-esteem in some way, this is attachment. Of course we may have demands for a child purely out of a wish for their happiness, but insisting that our children show strengths that are beyond them is attachment and paves the way for worry. Our children need to find a self-acceptance which is not conditional on their performance. In today's competitive school environment, this is a lot to ask for, but we can help by accepting 'what is' and praising our children's best efforts.

Meditate

Again, as with anger, an antidote to worry is to meditate, if only to give our minds a break. Like re-booting a computer when it starts to misbehave, we can return more calmly to our lives with a fresh mental screen. When we worry we must strive to keep our minds in the present for the present is all we can control—a mindfulness meditation on the breath is the best way to practise concentrating on the here and now. Worrying makes our world so small and meditation is a way to create spaciousness, to connect with a world so much greater than the constricted one we have created for ourselves. We realise that life is so much larger than this transitory problem.

It's easy to become stuck in a narrow perspective of our problem. We become so used to thinking about our problem on an intellectual level, racing off on umpteen different fantasies and trains of thought that we forget to question our view of a problem, and our approach to it. Often, we bring so much emotional baggage to a situation that we overlook the bare facts. Meditation can help with this by giving us space to look deeply into our problem from a position of stillness and concentration. Part of this 'looking deeply' is to question all our beliefs and thoughts around the problem rather than taking them as givens. By asking ourselves questions such as, 'What are the results of my current approach to the problem?' and 'How trapped am I really?', we can be creative in seeking alternatives. When our mind wanders we can bring it back to our breath to make it still and spacious before recommencing our enquiry.

When our worry makes us feel sad, panicked or helpless, when it feels like a solid object, a 'thing' that saps our energy and well-being, it helps if we use our breath to calm ourselves. Subhana Barzaghi is a mother of three boys, a Zen teacher and psychotherapist. She recommends taking some time to breathe with the worry: identify where in your body the tension from this worry is collecting; focus your attention on that point and as you breathe out, release the tension. On every out-breath visualise yourself letting go of more of the tension and negativity that's causing you to suffer. Subhana claims this practice will 'take the edge off' the intensity of your feelings.

Smile

It also helps enormously to smile as often as possible, especially when you catch yourself worrying. Some meditators aim to smile as they meditate just as the Buddha does. Others remind themselves to smile throughout the day. Try smiling to yourself right now and watch the subtle effect it has on your mind or any tension in your body. Try smiling more during conversations and notice how much happier you feel.

When your worst fears come true

How can Buddhism help us when our fears and worries are well-founded? Sometimes, it's no longer a matter of examining our thoughts to discover how much of our suffering we are creating: the suffering is there—undeniable and close enough to unbearable. Your child may be seriously ill, struggling at school or suffering hardships in the playground. In the popular parenting magazine

Sydney's Child, an article appeared in March 2001 that had many a mother talking. Titled 'When They Were Bad—My Daughter is Exiled and We Suffer a Season in Hell', the mother writes of her daughter's first year at high school: 'She went from being a member of the "in crowd" to becoming its designated exile. She was talked about, hated, despised, not invited, ridiculed—but mostly, most cruelly ignored.'

The story describes the stream of nasty emails, a friendless school holiday, a daughter waking up 'sick' and not wanting to go to school. How could a mother not be beside herself with fear and worry? The mother writes: 'I slowly lost myself. I avoided friends, didn't go to parties and suffered along with her. How long could it last? How long could we last?'

It lasted the whole year until finally the daughter changed schools and her problems were over. What did the mother learn from this nightmare? In her own words: 'There is no immunisation against hurt. There is no protection against cruelty. For all the things I can do for her, saving my daughter from life's hard twists is not one of them. Tough lesson all the way round.'

At these times we acknowledge the first Noble Truth: that there is suffering and dissatisfaction. There's no point in trying to cheer ourselves up or distract ourselves from the pain. We have no choice but to face the most unpleasant of emotions. One of the wiser clichés captures this: if we can't go round it, we have to go through it. One consolation that Buddhist teachings emphasise is that in experiencing such suffering we deepen our potential for compassion towards others who suffer. In this story the daughter soon became a sensitive confidante to the next victim at her former school. And the mother, who had also experienced bullying in her school years, was better able to comfort her daughter through this difficult period.

The other consolation that Buddhism can offer in such times is the teaching of impermanence. As expressed in Buddhist scriptures in the *Songs of Milarepa*:

Do you not fear the miseries
You experienced in the past?
Surely you will feel much pain
If misfortunes attack you?
The woes of life succeed one another
Like the sea's incessant waves—
One has barely passed, before
The next one takes its place

No matter what we experience it will pass. Not only that, it will change form and vary in intensity. For the daughter the bullying did ease after its initial intensity, not enough for her to want to stay at the school, but as with all forms of suffering, its nature kept changing form before finally passing away.

Lyn is a Buddhist mother of three boys. She notes that with her first son she agonised over every problem that arose, be it feeding, achieving milestones or coping with school. She was often pleasantly surprised that each problem worked itself out and eventually dissolved altogether. She felt far more relaxed on meeting problems with her second son and jokes that by the third, she felt little need to worry at all. With hindsight she wonders why she ever worried about some of the issues at all.

The words of Myla Kabat-Zinn, who has raised three children, can encourage us too. With her Buddhist husband she co-wrote *Everyday Blessings, The Inner Work of Mindful Parenting*, which emphasises how much we can help our children just by accepting them for exactly who they are. Arguing that we need to accept even characteristics we find challenging, Myla writes: 'Children can face all sorts of difficulties and challenges if they can come back to the well of our unconditional love. For it is in our honoring of their whole selves that inner growth and healing take place.'

Listening to our children

When I was pregnant with my firstborn I naively did a course to become a volunteer telephone counsellor. It was naive because as a breast-feeding mother I would never be available to attend the four-hour shifts required, apart from the fact that family life rarely affords mothers such stretches of time. Before Zac's arrival, I did manage to complete the course and do about ten shifts and this gave me an opportunity to learn some principles of effective listening. Later, reading parenting books I found the exact principles reiterated and they all resonated with Buddhist teachings.

Listening can be a form of meditation requiring concentration, restraint and a degree of silence. Using the attention-without-comment approach that we practise in formal meditation, we keep our thoughts and opinions out of the process as much as we can so that we can focus on the speaker's version of reality. When children express emotions like sadness or anger, they give you a chance to become a confidante, a chance to teach them that emotions are normal and that there are constructive ways to deal with negative feelings. When they later face the weightier challenges of adolescence, you will be a proven ally. One mother of two claims that listening attentively to her children has been the most helpful part of her Buddhist practice.

Finding time is always an issue if we are to listen to our children mindfully. Along with the need for openness and patience on our part, we also need some control over the noise level around us and the presence of other demanding children. Yet the effort required to achieve these conditions pays off in the long-term. When a parent allows a child to experience a full emotional range, the child can develop normally without suppressing the unpleasant and without shutting down emotionally.

Listen without judging

Sometimes the problems that upset a child are, to adults, ridiculous. But whether it's a monster in the wardrobe or the boy next door stealing pencils, the issues feel serious to a child. We need to suspend our adult perspective and consider the problem from a child's viewpoint, to enter their inner world and try to understand its intensity. When we say, 'Don't be silly' or 'Don't be so sensitive', when we dismiss their concerns, the child feels as though their version of reality is irrelevant or unimportant.

Allow them to talk it through

When your child is upset, indulge them with uninterrupted talking time. Say little and prompt them—'Go on', 'Uh huh'—or be silent for them. It's difficult to avoid the temptation to interrupt or jump in with an instant solution, but your child needs to feel heard. Delay introducing your own opinions or experiences—'That reminds me of the time I . . .' and keep the focus on your child's problem: too many children stop confiding in parents who hijack their talking time.

Let them feel understood

Rather than feed your child a string of questions, paraphrase what they've said—restate the gist of what your child has said, using your own words, without adding your own comments. For example:

> Child: It was my cricket bat, but they wouldn't let me use it. All the other kids used my bat but I didn't even touch it.
> Parent: So they wouldn't let you have your turn.

This child would feel understood and free to continue with what they want to say rather than having to answer a question.

Concentrate on feelings

Children have a right to their feelings no matter how intense or how socially unacceptable. We need to convey the message that there are no wrong feelings, only wrong behaviours. The greater their vocabulary for feelings, the more they become capable of communicating negative emotions and diagnosing their own problems.

To help our children feel understood, we can reflect their feelings back to them. We can use the following list of synonyms for four key emotional states to help our children find the right word to express how they're feeling—'It sounds like you're feeling . . .'

Angry	**Sad**	**Stressed**	**Confused**
Frustrated	Rejected	Panic stricken	Disoriented
Upset	Devastated	Threatened	Muddled
Mad	Hopeless	Nervous	Mixed up
Furious	Hurt	Shocked	Worried
Irritated	Depressed	Stunned	Lost
Disturbed	Flat	Agitated	Trapped
Annoyed	Miserable	Tense	Unsure
Fuming	Crushed	Edgy	Uncertain
Bothered	Low	Anxious	Insecure
Cranky	Down	Uneasy	Overwhelmed
Neglected	Weepy	Helpless	Undecided
Misunderstood	Empty	Negative	Blank

Allow them to solve their own problems

Let your child decide how they're going to solve a problem, even though it will often be easier to simply tell them what to do. Although you are there to guide them and offer suggestions, give them as much control of the process as they are capable of dealing with. This will make them more competent problem solvers for the times you can't be there. Ask your child:

- What do you think you should do?
- What will you do if that doesn't work?
- What have you tried before?

Test options against the values you try to cultivate for your family. Is this solution fair? Honest? Considerate to others? Would anyone be hurt? Keep in mind though, that problem solving happens only after you have listened to your child and explored their feelings. It's frustrating when someone tries to solve our problem before we've finished explaining it.

Practise mindfulness. Monitor your own feelings and reactions and ask, 'What is required of me in this moment?' In particular, ask, 'Should I talk or should I remain silent?' We need to be vigilant with ourselves and learn from our mistakes, and it helps if we reflect on the conversation later and ask ourselves, 'Did I interrupt?' 'Did I talk too much before hearing everything my child had to say?' 'Did I jump in and fix the problem before giving my child a chance?'

Suffering makes us stronger

Living a spiritual life might seem relatively easy when our lives are going along swimmingly. On those days when the problems are few and the joys are many, we're in good form and our practice may flow more easily. It might take a bout of suffering to see how much we have really progressed along the spiritual path. It's during the hard times that we have the best opportunities to learn about ourselves and develop self-awareness. And there is no more testing time than when our children suffer.

In *A Path with Heart*, Jack Kornfield provides these words of encouragement for suffering parents:

> Spiritual life becomes more genuine when things become more difficult. Our children have inevitable accidents and illnesses. Tragedies occur. These situations call for a constancy of our love and wisdom. Through them we touch the marrow of practice and find our true spiritual strength.

With the demands of domestic life we may lament our lack of time for formal spiritual practice. Let's not forget though, family life, if we exploit it, is spiritual practice of the most valuable kind.

What we can do

- Realise the need to manage the worrying mind so that it doesn't affect our children.
- Remember that the more you worry, the more you worry. Every thought has a karmic effect.
- Consider writing as a way to consciously explore and manage your worries.
- Write a list of positive thoughts to counter-attack those that fuel your worries.
- Accept some suffering as a natural part of life, realising that aversion or battling against the suffering can be more painful than the suffering itself.
- Watch your thoughts and notice when they are snowballing or distorting.
- Be aware when you pay 'inappropriate attention' and use your will power to stop it.
- Identify any unhelpful beliefs, such as, 'My child mustn't suffer.'
- Become aware of your (unconscious) demands and try to convert them to milder preferences.
- Meditate to create space and take the edge off your tension.
- Explore your worries using mindful investigation, observing whatever comes up and remaining open to new directions.

- Smile. Whenever.
- No matter what you experience it will change form, vary in intensity and pass.
- Listen to your children without judging—allow them to talk things through; let them feel understood; concentrate on feelings; and allow them to solve their own problems.
- Remember that suffering has the potential to enrich our spiritual life.

Chapter 6

creating *loving* relationships

NOTHING LASTS. ALL IS transitory or in the process of change. This is especially evident when we contemplate how becoming a parent changes our relationships with our friends and family. Relationships that seemed to have settled into a fixed rhythm over the years become open to major shifts and transformations. With our parents and in-laws there's potential for all kinds of changes. We may see them far more frequently, or in some cases, less. Their response to our children and to our new role may give us cause for gratitude, or resentment. We may suffer from that well-known syndrome whereby 'grandparents and grandchildren unite against the common foe'—us.

Our friendships with those who don't have children often suffer from our parenting responsibilities. Children rob us of time we used to give such friends, interrupting our conversations and rarely letting us talk on the phone. We might find the nature of these friendships changes dramatically—how much interest can we expect friends without children to take in the details of mothering? A friendship must be strong to survive children. Some old friends vanish, others might fade out of our lives gradually. Both situations can be painful for us—and for our old friends.

Our relationships with fellow parents may deepen as we enjoy our shared interest in parenting. A special bond develops as our children enjoy playing together and as we provide support and companionship for each other. Yet we may also find with fellow parents new ground for being competitive, judgemental or jealous. After all, each of us makes different decisions about the role of career, the importance of relationships outside our family and how we raise our children. Many find it difficult to respect the decisions other mothers make and to be tolerant of their different values.

Then, most importantly, there's our relationship with our immediate family. Our relationship with our partner merits a chapter of its own (see Chapter 7), and we know how significant our children are. To say they are our spiritual teachers is an understatement. They are more like resident Zen Masters, constantly yanking us back into the present moment, setting us problems to solve and forcing us to question our assumptions. It's like they were sent to challenge our every expectation, opinion and character trait. They are the best teachers available when it comes to showing us that nothing lasts: no sooner do we feel we have a handle on our relationship with them, than they present new challenges or they've entered their next phase.

Relationships provide excellent training ground for Buddhist teachings. We could fool ourselves that we are growing wiser with the years but only through our relationships can we test whether such a hunch is correct. Relationships show us how well our practice is working. The people in our lives are all our spiritual teachers. If we examine the way we act towards others, what we say to them and how we think about them, they become walking report cards telling us whether our thoughts are as patient, kind and honest as we like to believe, and whether our thoughts are free from greed, hatred and delusion.

Attachment to our views and judgements

Thrust into parenthood, we find that many of our assumptions about life are thrown into flux, from our views about who we are and what we are capable of, to our opinions about child-raising and a whole range of other issues. As my friend Joanne puts it: 'I found a humility that reminds me that despite what I thought I knew, I really don't know much about anything anymore, except that Tinky-Winky, Dipsy, La-la and Po love each other very much.' From a Buddhist perspective, this process of reshaping or discarding old ideas is useful, for grasping onto our views and judgements leads to as much suffering as any other attachment. It doesn't mean we shouldn't have any opinions, rather that we will suffer if we cling to them in a grasping, needy way.

As with all episodes in our lives, there's potential for our minds to become smaller and meaner through the experience of parenting. When we feel tired and ragged, as mothers often do, we are less likely to see the best in others and it's easier to work ourselves into states of anger and delusion. We might, for example, find ourselves judging other mothers: 'She works long hours—that explains why her children behave so badly'; 'She doesn't work—she's got it easy'; 'She's too strict—that's why her children never seem happy'; or 'She's not strict enough—that's why her children always run amok'.

If we take a moment to imagine someone making any of these statements about ourselves, we could easily defend ourselves with a multitude of reasonable explanations, as could any mother falling victim to such judgements. Our situations are so complex that rarely can an outsider make a fair judgement. An observer can't know what kind of day a mother is having, how much support she receives or what the intentions behind her actions are. Neither can an observer know the family background influencing a mother's behaviour, how much sleep she is lacking or her emotional state.

Too often we hear about long-term friendships falling apart over different parenting styles. This tends to happen when mothers are attached to their own opinions and views. In Buddhism, there's nothing wrong with holding views, but if we identify too strongly with them, if we allow them to define who we are, if we use them to justify treating others in unloving ways, then we suffer from attachment. And as the second Noble Truth explains, attachment causes unhappiness.

At first I was surprised that Buddhism could teach that attachment to our views could be perilous. Our Western education encourages us to debate, take a stand and defend it—this makes us look strong and well-informed. Without views and firm opinions we may feel like a nobody—we tend to find some identity in holding views. Interestingly, holding views is also a convenient way to justify our negative feelings for others and so separate ourselves from them. Commenting on the widespread tendency for parents to judge each other, a wise friend remarked, 'What a perfect world we'd live in if all kids were raised by their next-door neighbours.'

Through Buddhism I've realised that many of the trouble spots I've experienced with friends over the years have been due to an insensitive clinging to my own views. In situations where restraint would have been the wisest option, I've felt compelled to express my opinion, often trampling over a friend's feelings. In defense of a cherished belief, I've failed to listen with openness to others or I've hastily expressed a view without regard for the complexities of the situation.

Now, as parents, we feel ourselves entitled to a whole new range of strong views. I find myself nitpicking about parents whose children are allowed to consume excessive amounts of junk food. But when I judge a parent whose children overindulge I may ignore the fact that the mother is suffering sleep deprivation, a cold or a rough week. Besides, junk food is not *completely* or *always* 'bad', so why cling to my view as if it were some sacred law? (Not to mention the fact that during the more testing weeks my own reliance on 'treats' can escalate and not to mention my own tendency to binge daily on chocolate.) By judging other parents I have a gratifying moment of self-righteousness but have strayed far from my goal of becoming tolerant, patient and understanding.

I can keep my opinions about junk food, but if I cling to them to define myself and alienate others they do me more harm than good. Buddhism encourages us to be open-minded, bringing the innocence of a child, rather than the prejudice of an adult, to each new situation. We need to be open to the multiplicity of questions in life, the mysteries rather than the 'facts'. In meditation and in mindful living we practise the skill of refusing to judge and rate, refusing to dredge up a tired old opinion, an automatic reaction.

Rather than assess and evaluate other parents, a compassionate response would be to give them the benefit of the doubt, as we so ardently hope they'll do for us when we are less than perfect. As experienced mothers often claim, one child can present twice as many challenges as another and all children are different, so we can't live in a world where all mothers parent in the same way.

Buddhist teachings urge us to use our own experiences to learn and grow. When we catch ourselves having judgemental thoughts we need to adopt an investigative attitude and look deeper. We need to be brutally honest as we ask ourselves the big questions. Why am I allowing this person to make my heart and mind contract? Does she remind me of issues that I struggle with or issues that I'd rather not address? Am I being competitive? What lesson should I be learning from this relationship? How can I transform my negative feelings into compassion?

Attachment to our friends and loved ones

The Buddha taught that attachment is the cause of our suffering and unhappiness. This is especially true for our relationships. Attachment makes any good intentions towards others conditional: when someone fails to conform to our rigid expectations, our feelings of friendliness dry up. We hold unspoken demands, expect people to somehow sense these, and then feel bitterly disappointed when they let us down. Neither loving nor caring, attachment fails to nourish our wish for others to be happy. Instead, it makes us clingy and needy.

Real love is motivated by a wish that others be happy and overcome suffering. It is unconditional: the way someone treats you doesn't affect your response of compassion. If this seems irrational, we need only think of our children, who can behave abominably all day and even profess hatred for us, yet we still love them intensely.

At worst, attachment makes us possessive as we harbour feelings of ownership: she's 'mine' and I must guard this relationship from all threats. We might insist people be the same as us, that they share the same views, interests and tastes. We might try to control them and before long we can't believe how negatively we feel towards a former source of joy. Real love, on the other hand, provides space and freedom for our friends and family to be themselves.

When we feel attachment, we see our friends as sources of our own happiness rather than people in their own right, but how fair or reasonable is it to make others responsible for our happiness?

Relationships, like all phenomena, are characterised by impermanence. They constantly change, just as each individual in a relationship is not a consistent, stable entity. Relying too much on other people for our happiness leads to unhappiness. We need to live with others in a non-demanding, self-sufficient way. If we could stop clinging to our relationships our minds would become more peaceful, freeing us from much anxiety, worry and fear.

As mothers, we need to be particularly careful that we check our love for our children for attachment. This means encouraging them to be themselves and loving them for who they are rather than what we graspingly hope they might become. We strive to see our children not through the veils of our fears, hopes and needs but with an attitude of acceptance. We avoid pegging our self-esteem to their performance and we check that our acceptance of them is not conditional on their talents, preferences and character traits.

Some parents expect their children to fulfil the dreams they never achieved—you can see this tendency reach extremes at children's sports events. Rather, we need to see our children not so much as under-our-control as in-our-protection, and only for a short time at that. As this mother of a three-year-old boy points out:

> I used to feel very territorial about raising my son. I resented any friends or relations telling him what to do. I felt insulted if anyone told him to say please, to stop being rough, to speak more quietly—that was my job thank you very much! Being divorced too I've really struggled to accept that my ex-husband will have some input in raising our son. It can't be all my way, all my rules.
>
> I've come to understand over time that I don't *own* my son. He's not my property. He in fact belongs to a community of people who love him and want the best for him. People who have just as much right as me to teach him about consideration of others and what is appropriate behaviour.

I've managed to let go somewhat and allow him to be raised by all the people who care about him.

The importance of love

The only point on which all religions agree is the need for love and kindness towards our fellow beings. Jesus said, 'Love one another as I have loved you.' In the Koran we find, 'No one of you is a believer until he desires for his brother that which he desires for himself.' Buddha said, 'So with a boundless heart should one cherish all living beings.' In Buddhism, love is defined as a genuine wish that others be happy and free from suffering and disquiet. Love is an energy which we can use as fuel for our intentions.

The Buddha pronounced 11 benefits that come from achieving a mind of loving kindness (see Appendix 4 for more of what the Buddha said about loving kindness):

1. You will sleep easily.
2. You will wake easily.
3. You will have pleasant dreams.
4. People will love you.
5. Celestial beings and animals will love you.
6. Celestial beings will protect you.
7. External dangers will not harm you.
8. Your face will be radiant.
9. Your mind will be serene.
10. You will die unconfused.
11. You will be reborn in happy realms.

In a nutshell, a mind of love leads to more restful sleep, love in return, protection and serenity. With so many benefits to living lovingly, you could argue that a compassionate life is in fact a selfish one and anything but self-sacrificing. Over time, we begin to understand how much joy is available to a loving mind.

Love produces a positive atmosphere, helping us feel more peaceful and happy. People close to us appreciate us more. People who once disliked us begin to warm to us. We seem to attract more friends as people trust us and feel comfortable with us. Our compassion for the suffering of others allows us to feel more connected with everyone. And more opportunities to experience joy arise as we become more capable of sympathetic joy for anyone with some good news.

To live lovingly simplifies our lives by purifying our minds and removing much of the guilt, anger and stress from our relationships. We experience mental stability as we spend less time thinking about ourselves. Our own problems begin to fade in significance and we discover mental clarity and improved concentration. We become less petty, judgemental and fault-finding as we grow more interested in the well-being of others. According to Buddhism, this leads to enhanced self-respect and confidence, and with these we can expect to find within ourselves more courage, resilience and determination, as this mother finds:

> To be loving and compassionate does not come naturally to me. I've developed the habit of picking faults in others and this troubles me. When I chat to those close to me I notice that a large proportion of my conversation is critical of others, petty too. When I catch myself caught up in negative thoughts about others I feel small-minded, mean and not very proud of myself.
>
> Practising loving kindness in meditation and daily life helps me transform my fault-finding mind into a mind that is more spacious, accepting and loving. With this more positive mind I can't help but like myself better and this makes me more confident in everything I do.

With minds of love, we progress smoothly along our spiritual path and life becomes a wholly different experience. Happiness, according to Buddhism, comes from caring for others. To quote Robert Thurman, author of *Inner Revolution*, father of five and the first Westerner to be ordained in the Tibetan tradition: 'I become an ever happier being in my unconcern for my self.' So the more people we value, the more happiness we can feel. Full of love, there is less space for feelings of emptiness, isolation or aimlessness.

The Four Divine Abodes

So, how can we check that our love for others is pure and free from attachment? What are the features of this purer form of love? The Buddha claimed that real love has four qualities: *loving kindness*, *compassion*, *sympathetic joy* and *equanimity*. These four divine dwelling places are interdependent and overlapping, acting like a system of checks and balances that help us question whether our love for others is genuine.

Loving kindness

The words 'loving kindness' come from the Pali term 'metta', often translated as 'unrestrained friendliness'. Loving kindness is an energy within ourselves that we can nurture until our capacity to love multiplies (to this end Buddhists practise the loving kindness meditation explained in Chapter 9). To progress on our path out of unhappiness and into wisdom, we need to develop a mind that wishes, 'May all beings be happy and free from suffering.' The Buddha urged us to wish for the happiness of not only our family and friends but all the people we know, the people we don't know and even the ones we find difficult.

This mother specialises in practising loving kindness towards all the children she meets rather than only her own:

> It's easy to fall into the trap of only noticing your own children to the point where the needs of other kids become invisible. I think mothers feel really grateful when I show care and

concern for their children. To chat to their kids, get to know them, allow them to feel comfortable with me—this is my way of practising loving kindness. We all want our children to grow up in a nurturing community with as many loving adults around them as possible. We feel touched when our friends show interest and appreciation for our children and it takes so little effort.

Thinking back on my own childhood, I feel enormous gratitude to the small handful of adults who, without being in any way related to me, went out of their way to take an interest in me and make me feel special. Their kindness really contributed to my self-confidence.

Importantly, when we act with loving kindness, we don't expect anything in return and, again, being mothers has taught us the art of giving without expecting a reward. When we practise loving kindness, the way people react to us becomes irrelevant, for the joy of having a loving mind is the only reward we need. In our own times of trouble we seek courage within rather than payback from all the people we've been kind to, as this inspiring verse by Adam Lindsay Gordon depicts:

Life is mostly froth and bubble
Two things stand like stone
Kindness in another's trouble
Courage in your own.

In short, we act kindly because, along with courage, kindness is the most important quality.

This treasure of a mother explains the role of loving kindness in her day:

I socialise a lot as a mother because I appreciate the adult company and I like to get out of the house. Spending time with other mothers gives me plenty of opportunities to practise loving kindness and I've found there's so many ways to be helpful. It could be minding a child here, offering some food there or putting up my hand to help at local playgroups and preschools. I organise lots of get-togethers in parks and cafes in the hope that the mothers I know can feel like they belong to a supportive community.

It's been interesting looking at my motives for all these activities. I feel better about myself when I help others out of a spirit of loving kindness rather than thoughts of what's in it for me, like say: if I babysit for her, she might help me out some time. It sounds pathetic and it's embarrassing to admit but I feel my motives for helping others have sometimes been a matter of, 'if I help her she'll think well of me and like me more'. And I guess I used to help people to reassure myself that I was a 'good' person. With my focus now on loving kindness, helping is much more about the other person than about me and ironically, this makes me feel happier. Still, on the selfish side, I know I'm looking after my karma when I consider the needs of others.

As I mentioned, loving kindness is sometimes translated as unrestrained friendliness. We all know *how* to be friendly, so there's little we need to actually learn. We know the power of a smile, a touch, some praise. The challenge is to remember to be friendly and to be open to the potential for friendliness in each moment. We need to challenge ourselves frequently, 'Is there anything I can do to help this person feel happier? To relieve some of their suffering?'

When we consider the role of loving kindness in our relationships, the importance of listening becomes clear. To help someone we need to be able to look deeply into their life. This requires us to take a keen interest in lives other than our own, to spend more time thinking about how others think and feel. If we aren't aware of what others might need it's possible our efforts to help them could do more damage than good. Looking deeply into the lives of those around us ensures our efforts to help don't turn us into interfering nuisances.

On this note, I cringe when I remember a couple of mothers turning down my offers of help. Seeking company for my son and hoping that I was practising loving kindness in giving the mothers a break, I offered to mind their children. But I was in fact being quite insensitive. The mothers had only met me a few times and hadn't met my husband, so my offer probably made them feel awkward and uncomfortable. But not least, the children were not even particularly familiar with me—how would they feel about being left in an unfamiliar house with a relative stranger? Buddhism encourages us to offer help sensitively, skilfully.

It's worth considering from time to time, how much love we send out into the world. Absorbed in our own thoughts we forget the potential in each day for moments of kindness. We fail to acknowledge the people around us, we overlook the small ways we can make others feel connected or even special. We all have power to reassure and honour the dignity of other living beings. To use Mother Teresa's wise and oft-quoted words: 'There can be no great acts, only small acts of great love.'

Compassion

Compassion is the impulse to relieve another's pain. To live with compassion for others is a matter of understanding the first Noble Truth and acknowledging the suffering or unhappiness that every living being must experience. As this Buddhist mother puts it:

> Learning the importance of compassion has worked wonders for all my relationships. No matter what kind of relationship difficulty I'm experiencing, if I can remember that this person suffers and if I can dwell for a while on what their suffering must be like, then compassion is the only response.

At the same time, compassion isn't about 'feeling sorry' for people, in the sense of a patronising form of pity, but rather a recognition that we're all in this together, we all seek happiness and freedom from suffering.

The Buddha taught us about the illusion of the separate self and that if we could see how we are all one, despite separate physical bodies, then helping others overcome their pain would come naturally. As mothers we experience this oneness with our children: to see our children in distress is to feel their pain and rush to their aid as if we ourselves needed help. This feels only natural with our children, and it's this compassionate response that we can aim to bring to other relationships too.

When we are in touch with our own pain, as Buddhism encourages us to be, we can respond more sensitively to the pain of others. If when we are in pain we frantically seek distractions, we are likely to treat the pain of others in the same way, encouraging them to magically 'cheer up' without acknowledging their feelings. On becoming a mother I suddenly became grateful for any hard times I'd survived at school. When a mother has experienced bullying, group politics or disappointing marks she can better understand what her child suffers in these situations.

To be compassionate we need to become mentally involved with the lives of others and never dismiss their concerns. When we judge someone's pain as an overreaction or as not really important (or interesting), we close the door on compassion. It's easy to see others' concerns as trivial and respond dismissively: 'Don't worry about that', 'Cheer up'. But such responses rarely help someone in distress. We all want to feel as if our story has been heard and our feelings understood. Dismissing another's pain shows a reluctance to acknowledge the first Noble Truth that there is suffering, that life is full of imperfection.

A Buddhist mother who agreed with this point said:

> I was always accusing my children of crying for no reason. Denying their pain I tended to respond, 'Don't be silly' or, 'C'mon, that didn't hurt'. Of course there are times when such statements are valid but I'm sure I overused them as a way to avoid confronting their suffering. I'm now challenging myself to look more deeply into their pain and respond more sensitively.

At that testing stage of motherhood when we must deal with tantrums we can remind ourselves to include compassion in our response. The experts tell us that a toddler's tantrum is born out of their frustration at not being able to express themselves—they don't have the words so resort to tears and screams. They feel powerless and don't have the life skills to deal with such unpleasant feelings. They don't know what to do when they're overtired. They don't understand why they can't have their way. All they know is that it all feels awful, even unbearable.

As mothers coping with these outbursts we may feel angry, frustrated, depressed and—if the tantrum is a public one—humiliated, but compassion for the suffering child could temper our response. And, who would deny there's a place for compassion at every stage of our children's development? I love the words of Myla Kabat-Zinn when she says in *Everyday Blessings*:

> When a child, no matter how old, feels our acceptance, when he feels our love, not just for his easy-to-live-with, lovable, attractive self, but also for his difficult, repulsive, exasperating self, it feeds him and frees him to become more balanced and whole.

One morning my Zac treated me to several hours of his more 'difficult, repulsive, exasperating self', defying me at every point of the effort to prepare for preschool. Later in the day his preschool phoned me to announce he had chicken pox and I found myself wishing that I'd been more patient with him that morning. Often enough their misbehaviour is quite understandable, if we can only be mindful of their point of view, or give them the benefit of the doubt. Maybe they're suffering from a change in their routine, a lack of attention, confusion about their boundaries. Maybe they're just tired and out-of-sorts. Myla Kabat-Zinn is not saying we put up with unacceptable behaviour. We just need to be mindful of what might be going on from our child's point of view, and factor compassion into our response, rather than react automatically and unthinkingly.

Family, friends and children aside, compassion towards ourselves is the foundation for any compassion towards others. If we let ourselves become tired and run-down caring for others we have less to give everyone. We need to look after our own health too by making time for quietness and rest. In practising compassion we speak kindly to ourselves and notice whether our inner voices are supportive and friendly or judgemental and demanding. We are patient when we falter, for parenting makes amateurs of us all as we confront its never-ending new stages. It helps to cultivate self-awareness, not guilt.

Sympathetic joy

Imagine how much happier we could be if we could share the joys experienced by each living being. Or, as the Dalai Lama put it, our chances of delight would be 'enhanced six billion to one'. Mothers are true masters of sympathetic joy when it comes to our children. There is no sweeter taste than our child's success and happiness. Think back to the joy we experienced at each stage that our child gradually learned to walk, talk and interact. Or consider how our hearts warm when we watch their delight at a swimming pool, a birthday party or on a trampoline. Their joys can give us bliss.

Once again we can learn from our love for our children more about how to love others. How often, for example, do we enjoy the victories of children other than our own? For that matter, how often do we celebrate the happiness of other adults? How do we feel when we hear about their good news? Jubilant? Or jealous and pressured to keep step? Can we bring ourselves to celebrate their feelings of relief, excitement and fulfilment?

Think how grateful we feel when a friend celebrates our good fortune with us in a heartfelt way. The friendship instantly deepens for it exemplifies and inspires the ultimate form of trust when we know our friend wants us to be happy. When we can rejoice in someone's good news we restore our sense of connection with others. How could we feel isolated when so emotionally involved in another's life?

If our friends fail to share our joys with us we are left asking ourselves, 'What's this friendship worth if they don't even want the best for me, if they don't understand what matters to me?' If we find it hard to feel happy for a joyful friend, it only means we need to look more deeply at the pain in their life, to understand their suffering. This mother learned exactly that:

> I've really been struggling with one of my friendships. A close friend has a daughter the same age as mine. I've always been very close to this woman but since we've both become mothers she's introduced this competitive element that I feel has poisoned our relationship. She's constantly comparing our daughters and it so happens that her daughter tends to come up looking better than mine. She walked earlier, talked earlier and now she's in school she seems to be the top of the class. My friend is constantly talking about her daughter's stunning achievements and I find it quite insensitive—especially when I'm a little worried about my own daughter's development in some areas. I can't believe how angry her insensitivity has made me and I even find myself resenting her daughter and wishing for her failure.
>
> Contemplating the four divine abodes, I knew I was falling down in the area of sympathetic joy. I have a perfect chance to celebrate a friend's good fortune in having a bright child but I've chosen to be jealous and angry. Rather than feel guilty and worthless, I'm trying to overcome my problem by cultivating compassion. For example, my friend has given up an impressive career to be a mother. She worries a lot about whether she'll be able to return to it and I know this sacrifice is a source of pain for her. Who could blame her for wanting to do a wonderful job at raising her daughter to make up for the career she's lost? Maybe her apparent boastfulness is a little insensitive but when I try to see it in context along with all her other problems as a mother and wife, I can feel compassion which helps me to share her happiness about her daughter.

The four Divine Abodes are interdependent such that you can't have one missing and still practise pure love. To experience true sympathetic joy we need to be capable of compassion. To share in a friend's pleasure we need also to share in their pain, otherwise we are fair-weather friends. When we understand the suffering in another's life it's only natural to feel joy when they find a pocket of happiness.

As with compassion, before we can feel sympathetic joy we need to listen attentively to others and be genuinely interested in them. Only then can we understand them deeply and know what makes them happy. We need to learn more about the people in our lives and, from time to time, ponder on what life might be like for them. Then we will be prepared to immerse ourselves in their happiness, exploring every delicious detail with them. This is offering true friendship.

Equanimity

In Chapter 3 we explored equanimity in some depth. In practising this quality—the ability to perceive all aspects of our lives with acceptance and patience—we avoid our usual extreme reactions. The product of a calm and unflappable mind, equanimity enables us to refuse to overreact to what is pleasant and what is not.

Again, the four Divine Abodes are interdependent and if we do not practise this fourth one our love is not complete. Without equanimity we might only undertake acts of loving kindness when we know we will be appreciated or the acts reciprocated. Without equanimity, we can only be compassionate when we know we won't be overwhelmed by another's pain. Without equanimity, sympathetic joy would give way to feelings of jealousy or competition.

In terms of the four Divine Abodes, the word equanimity includes the idea of seeing all living beings as equally precious. Within the family unit itself, for example, it's often easier for both mothers and fathers to show loving kindness, compassion and joy towards our children than to our partners. At the breakfast table my husband once (jokingly) brought to my attention the fact that though I had greeted my sons that morning like an overexcited puppy I had barely even glanced his way. As we've all seen, too many marriages and partnerships fall apart when a partner is no longer appreciated for who they are but only for their performance in their parenting role.

We are one

Living with *loving kindness*, *compassion*, *sympathetic joy* and *equanimity* would happen quite naturally if we could sense our interconnectedness with others, if we could understand that we are one with all living beings. Generosity, sensitivity and service can flow when we see those around us as parts of ourselves. As mothers we serve our children as though they are parts of ourselves: their comfort is our comfort. The challenge is to bring this kind of love and compassion to all our relationships until nobody is excluded. Vietnamese monk Thich Nhat Hanh writes:

> You and the object of your love cannot be two. Continue [meditating] until you see yourself in the cruellest person on Earth, in the child starving . . . in everyone in the supermarket, on the street corner, in a concentration camp.

To understand this *non-separation* is to rejoice in the happiness of others and share in their suffering, all the while feeling the joy of our oneness, our connectedness. Our concept of a self, separate from others, is a delusion, but we can't see our way out of this misconception until we awaken. When we realise the true nature of our existence our sense of isolation, separation and loneliness no longer haunts us.

Interestingly, the world of science, particularly physics, is often arriving at the same conclusions that the Buddha reached 2500 years ago. Albert Einstein, for example, explained the delusion of self and the truth of oneness:

> A human being is a part of the whole called by us 'the universe', a part limited in time and space. He experiences himself his thoughts and feelings as something separate from the rest—a kind of optical delusion of his consciousness. This delusion is a kind of prison for us, restricting us to our personal desires and affection for a few persons nearest to us. Our task must be to free ourselves from this prison by widening our circle of understanding and compassion to embrace all living creatures and the whole of nature in its beauty.

Zen teacher and mother of two Susan Murphy makes the point that we were not always caught up in this delusion of being separate, for as babies, we knew better:

> Babies are born with an awareness of the oneness of all creation. In their eyes, the stars and the vastness are still slowly turning. Just look into that mirror of your own original nature (you can't resist it anyway)—there it is! Naked awareness.
>
> Through a process of 'unlearning' they develop an eye that breaks the world down into parts, the whole-adapted eye becomes a part-adapted eye. We need to be able to see the world in its various parts in order to learn concepts and language, to communicate with others, but we then face the task of returning to a view of the world and ourselves as one connected whole.

Experienced meditators speak of how at a higher level of concentration they can catch a life-changing glimpse of this oneness with all living beings and even our oneness with all phenomena. Robert Thurman speaks of this glimpse of oneness that we can experience during meditation:

> We lose all sense of boundary, all tension of struggle, and experience . . . a realness that . . . seems to be connected to all

> other beings and things. This is the real self, an inexhaustible well of peace and happiness, incorporating all, fulfilling all desires, embracing all others without neglecting ourselves. This is the essence of what the Buddha saw during his own meditation.

Some find motherhood brings them closer to an understanding of oneness. As this mother put it:

> Looking into the face of my baby I saw glimpses of my mother and then my auntie and then a string of other relations. It gave me a sense of our interconnection and a flow of connection down through the generations. And through this baby I felt more connected to my husband, and his whole family through time, like we had found a way to merge ourselves into one being and tie ourselves together through a strengthened bond with each other.

On our way to this understanding of oneness, we can at least see that all living beings share the same wish for *happiness and freedom from suffering*. Buddhist teachings constantly emphasise this point. We're all in the same boat looking for the same thing and this natural camaraderie can help us to understand our oneness at least on an intellectual level, before we develop the deeper understanding available with spiritual progress.

Cleansing our relationships of attachment

Once we understand the effects of attachment, the way it fuels expectations, demands and neediness, we become amazed at its potential to poison our relationships. Replacing it with a purer form of love takes awareness of our intentions, thoughts and desires in relation to others. We need to be scrupulously honest with ourselves about the contents of the mind that drives our actions. Basically it comes down to the question, 'Am I doing/saying/thinking this out of love or for my own benefit?'

Even if we find our intentions and feelings are less than loving, we can at least start acting lovingly. When we act lovingly we notice how pleasurable this feels and this encourages us to think and feel in more loving ways. We are likely to find that the way people respond to our acts of love inspires us to act in a more heartfelt manner. When we act lovingly we notice benefits on many levels—practical, emotional, spiritual and physical—and before long it seems irrational to act any other way. Ironically, acting lovingly can work out to be quite self-serving.

To our loving acts we eventually add loving intentions and thoughts by actively cultivating a mind of love. Through loving kindness meditation, we practise fostering feelings of loving kindness towards others and, as we do so, transform the nature of our minds. We start to realise that with love we are capable of so much more than we ever thought possible and that life could become a completely different prospect. And as mothers, we have faith in the power of love because we have already experienced a revolution of our minds through loving our children.

What we can do

- Remember that everyone in your life is a spiritual teacher, especially your children. Learn from all your relationships.
- Consider holding your opinions more loosely to help reduce your own suffering and feel more connected to others.
- If you feel judgemental or critical of somebody, investigate your feelings mindfully. Difficult relationships often teach us the most.
- Examine all your relationships for signs of attachment. Do you expect people to meet your unspoken demands or agree with your views?
- Accept who your children are without projecting your own needs and insecurities onto them—we don't own our children, they are in our protection.
- Realise how important it is to love others and remember this helps to make you happier and clearer.
- Acknowledge that love has four components: loving kindness, compassion, sympathetic joy and equanimity.
- Work on realising that we are all one. This will help the four divine abodes to flow freely.
- Start acting lovingly and with time the right intentions will follow.

Chapter 7

living *with* partners

SCIENTISTS TELL US THE powerful chemicals activated when we fall in love wear off within 18 to 30 months. Under the influence of that initial passion, the relationship seems effortless and we are almost blind to our partner's flaws—just as they are to ours. But once we've shared our lives for a few years and had children, most relationships experience shaky times. For some couples the challenges strengthen their bond, others limp along barely surviving and some part company.

As always, the truth of impermanence, or the inevitability of change, is inescapable. Even those mothers who seem to live with their soul mates concede there are phases when they 'can't get enough' of their partners followed by phases when they could 'take them or leave them'. All relationships go through seasons. Yet in the heat of a battle, or during a difficult patch, it's easy to paint our whole history together in the same shade, generalising: 'I've never been happy with him', 'He's always in a bad mood', 'We never enjoy each other's company anymore'.

But it's not only the quality of our partnerships which constantly changes. We also need to be open to how our partners as individuals continue to develop, just as we ourselves do. It's unfair to cling to an outdated view of who our partner is, for just as we have no 'self' that behaves with perfect consistency, neither does our partner. (In Chapter 8 we look in detail at how clinging to a self-image puts us in the cage of our expectations.) In the same way, closing our minds to our partner's potential for change and inconsistency might stop us from listening to them with the attention that could so benefit both of us.

We can determine whether our feelings for our partner are truly loving by examining our love for signs of attachment and then revisiting the four Divine Abodes. Taking personal responsibility is essential also to success in relationships: are we both aware of the intentions behind our actions as well as how our behaviour affects each other? Skilful communication, both in our speech and our ability to listen mindfully, is another key ingredient in a good relationship.

If your partnership isn't as loving as it could be, it may be a question of initiative: one of us has to kick-start the improvement process. We can wait forever for our partner to behave differently or we can decide to introduce more loving behaviour ourselves. Then again, many mothers feel their partnership already suffers from an imbalance—they seem to be responsible for more acts of love and nurture in their relationships. Such women can still benefit from Buddhist teachings but might also consider finding ways to share them with their partners.

The family is a unit where imbalance in one relationship affects the other relationships within the organism: when our partnership is loving, our whole family is happier. Our children watch and learn from the relationship between their parents—the way we cope with tension, our manner of speaking to each other and the way we resolve conflict—so it is good for the whole family when we are aware of our way of relating to our partners rather than cruising in automatic.

The havoc children wreak on our love life

On the positive side, children provide our partnerships with a common interest to savour together. Children can symbolise a firm commitment to a shared future. As a couple, we share our delight in watching our children achieve all those developmental milestones. We laugh together at their wild antics, their quirky remarks. Gazing together into the face of our long-awaited newborn, rumbling with our excitable toddler, marvelling at their capacity to enjoy simple pleasures—these moments nourish our partnerships. Through all this we feel closer to our partner—these are the good times.

Still, the upheaval that children bring can lead either partner to feel resentful or even hostile about the relationship. The pressures that children put on our partnership are immense: they leave us with less time for each other; they rob us of sleep and energy; need constant attention and assistance; they interrupt our conversations—

they're always there! Many couples find themselves wondering what ever happened to satisfying conversation, shared interests, outings as a couple, romance and sex.

With children a couple faces a myriad of new issues. Joanne was a lawyer with a strong background in feminism before motherhood struck and reports:

> The snag in the sharing of parental responsibility was that when the baby cried it was my breasts, not my unsexist very-willing-to-help partner's the baby wanted. All the equality I had negotiated in my relationship waned; my partner and I slipped shamelessly into gender roles: motherhood taunted the feminist in me. For the first time in my life, the feminist did not know what to say.

Children multiply the housework which creates potential for conflict over allocating it fairly. A couple may argue vehemently over how best to raise a child, especially if they come from different types of families. Money, or the lack thereof, may cause stress through not only increased expenditure but often a decreased household income, as one of us reduces our hours of paid work. Our workplaces are slow to apply family-friendly policies, adding overtime and other forms of inflexibility to our difficulties.

In many households, the separate worlds of the parent who cares for the child(ren) and the parent who goes out to work can seem so far apart, as we find we have less in common and compete over who has the most difficult situation: 'You think you had a bad day! I had to put up with . . .' At worst, we find our relationships fall into a rut. We are caught in habits of snapping at each other, bickering and feeling resentful—and in many cases resign ourselves to this way of relating.

The Buddhist message 'stopping and realising' is of particular value for relationship problems. We need to stop and realise how we are relating to each other and acknowledge the existence of a more wholesome alternative. Our partnerships make excellent training grounds for developing spiritual virtues. We can reject harmful ways of relating—we have the choice. Partnership, like raising children, is just one more form of spiritual practice and the more we can see it in these terms, the more motivated we'll be to work at it.

If a partnership can survive children intact then it has survived the greatest of tests and is of great value. How can Buddhism help us achieve this near miracle?

Loving our partners more purely

To practise Buddhism we need to cultivate loving relationships with all living beings, and this includes our partner. To help us love our partners purely we need to check our relationships for attachment as well as the illusion of separation. We also need to ensure the presence of the four Divine Abodes: loving kindness, compassion, sympathetic joy and equanimity. As unenlightened beings we're likely to find we fall short in some of these areas, so life with our partner can only improve.

Love or attachment?

We know our relationship is one of unhealthy attachment when we find ourselves dwelling on our own needs and expectations and whether our partner fulfils them, and when we spend relatively little time considering life from our partner's point of view. We expect our partner to read our minds, discover what we want and make us happy. We might find ourselves thinking: 'If they really loved me, they'd do *x*, *y* and *z*.'

Contentment needs to come from within ourselves, so we can't expect our partner to be an enduring source of happiness. Sometimes, relationship troubles are partly due to our neglect of our own inner lives—a common trap in the busy household.

It is helpful to ask ourselves:

- Do we or our partner feel needy, clingy or emotionally dependent?

- Is our love rife with expectations and demands? Are our feelings towards each other conditional on these being met?
- Do we provide each other with enough space to evolve, change and grow?

Do we understand our oneness?

As mentioned in the last chapter, we labour under the delusion that we have a separate 'self' whose interests compete with those of 'others'. We overlook our essential connectedness. Even if we cannot understand the truth of our oneness with all living beings, we can at least acknowledge our shared desire for happiness and freedom from suffering. This gives the most dissimilar of individuals a significant point in common.

To examine the extent to which we feel as one with our partner, we can ask ourselves:

- Is our relationship plagued by a deluded sense of separation, disconnection, 'me' versus 'you'?
- Can we see that caring about each other's interests is a way of caring about ourselves?

For love to exist all four of the Divine Abodes must be present. We can ask ourselves the following questions to help us focus on the Divine Abodes:

Is there loving kindness?

- Do we both earnestly wish our partner to be happy and free from suffering or discomfort?
- Do we actively think of ways to be kind to each other, to give each other moments of happiness?
- Do we both express appreciation? What is the ratio of praise to criticism?
- Do we listen attentively to each other so we can understand our partner's world and their needs?

Is there compassion?

- How often do we contemplate the difficulties of our partner's situation?
- Do we both understand what makes the other suffer?
- Do we listen to each other's grievances and wish we could alleviate any pain?
- Do we regularly express an interest in, or inquire about each other's difficulties?
- Can we forgive each other for past mistakes?

Is there sympathetic joy?

- Are we happy for each other's joys? Can we celebrate together?
- Is there any jealousy or competition fuelled perhaps by resentment?
- Do we know enough about each other's lives to know what sources of joy might be?

Is there equanimity?

- Do we expect our partner to deliver everything we need? Or do we love many other people so that we don't unfairly depend on our partner to fulfil all our needs for connection with others?
- Can we accept the changing seasons of a relationship, that it's natural to have winters and that the springs will follow?

Taking responsibility

Through mindfully observing our reactions throughout a day we become aware of our tendency to chase what feels pleasurable and flee what doesn't. We might notice that it doesn't feel pleasurable to take responsibility for our less wholesome thoughts and behaviours towards our partner. We don't feel particularly comfortable admitting that we overreacted or that we were wrong. I know, for myself, the humble act of saying sorry is only for special occasions, even though it's unlikely that I make it through a week with a perfect record of selfless virtue.

Our natural response is to avoid facing our own responsibility. We distract ourselves from thinking about our own role in any tension: we can squash uncomfortable feelings of guilt by moving onto our next important task or watching a sitcom with a bowl of ice-cream. It's often easier to blame our partner even though we eventually find ourselves in a rut of resentment from which we never take the time to examine our own part. We know we're in that rut when all thoughts of our partner are negative, even though our partner is unlikely to be devoid of good qualities.

Taking responsibility is about 'stopping and realising'. Both partners need to stop and question whether their behaviour towards each other is skilful. Skilful behaviour reinforces love; unskilful behaviour reinforces a sense of separation. We all know how to behave skilfully: we take an interest, we give time and attention, we praise each other and find ways to make each other happy. Skilful behaviour is not something we need to learn so much as constantly realise the need for.

One Buddhist mother, Meredith, finds that when her husband is in a bad mood, her own reaction can plunge the household into conflict. Meredith is learning to take some responsibility for her role in the conflicts.

> If my husband has had a stressful day at work he can be dark and moody when he gets home. My knee-jerk reaction is to hate this and resent what he does to the atmosphere of our house with his glum face and his brooding. What I needed to face was that my refusal to accommodate his mood was doing as much damage to the atmosphere as his bad mood. By confronting him I inflamed his mood and dumped my own negative feelings into the atmosphere of the house. I needed to acknowledge firstly that bad moods are a natural part of life and that he has a right to one occasionally just as I do, and

secondly that his mood always passes and doesn't always need to be squashed on sight.

I needed to learn to restrain my own reactions and avoid the instant argument that could escalate the whole situation. Observing my reactions to his bad moods mindfully, I caught myself feeling hatred for my husband, demonising him for being less than perfect. I felt no compassion for the strain he was under—it's hard to come home from a gruelling day of work and devote yourself to a family.

It's not that I'm letting him get away with murder. There are times when the bad moods need to be addressed sensitively, ideally, when the children have gone to bed. He too needs to take responsibility for his behaviour at home. The point is that we both need to and that it can be destructive to paint myself as the eternally wronged victim who has to live with a monster.

Although there are inevitably times when your partner is at fault, if we take some of the responsibility for our difficulties, we can learn, grow and strengthen the relationship. It's rare that both parties are completely blameless. I know that when I need to address an issue with Marek, it disarms him if I can open by accepting some blame. I say, for example, 'I know I haven't yet managed to teach Zac about picking up his toys but when you're carrying the baby it's probably a good idea to watch your step.' Which is generally less provocative than, 'For god's sake watch where you're going!'

We need to examine the intentions behind our actions towards our partners. Can we expect good karma from our intentions or are they conditioning our hearts to become harder. And what are the effects of our actions—on ourselves and others? To take more responsibility is to learn to listen not only to the words you say but also to what you tell yourself about your relationship. It's also about recognising that you choose your responses—they are not inevitable.

There are days when we have to admit that only our own world and our own comfort matters to us, when we completely overlook our partner's experience of life. And there are days when they overlook our reality and, if this is too often, we need to sensitively choose a time to address the issue, choosing our words with care. The value of skilful speech cannot be overstated and later in this chapter we'll consider the words of the Buddha on this component of the Eightfold Path.

Loving ourselves

Whether or not we're aware of it, we often treat others in a similar way to how we treat ourselves. If we avoid exploring our own pain, we don't tend to look deeply at the pain of others. If we are harsh and judgemental with ourselves, this can extend to others as well. Compassion towards ourselves is therefore the foundation for compassion in all our relationships, including our partnership. Moreover, if we lack compassion for ourselves we may feel needy or demanding towards our partner. We may expect our partner to become the source of what we fail to provide ourselves.

Buddhism offers several ideas on how to develop self-love. During loving kindness meditation or throughout the day we can learn to recall our own goodness. We bring to mind a past act of generosity and discover a compelling reason to love ourselves more. We remind ourselves of our capacity for love and find a source of pride as we interrupt our usual flow of more critical self-judgements. We may have learned that to love ourselves we must be 'good' enough, we must excel in a particular area or we must be loved by others. It feels liberating when you can switch the focus to loving yourself because you minded your neighbour's children or felt compassion for someone suffering or helped someone in need.

Another way to foster self-love is to meditate on or simply remind ourselves of our own Buddha Nature. We are all free to acknowledge that a perfectly loving and wise being dwells within each of us. When we're in touch with our Buddha Nature and the love it can lavish on us and others, we have less need for our partner to show love for us in prescribed ways.

Many of us feel disappointed that our partners fail to provide the kind of love we feel we need. Our partners may not satisfy us in the areas of talking intimately, showing care and consideration or providing non-sexual affection. The problem may not be a lack of love in the hearts of our partners so much as a failure to express it in the way we crave. Sourcing love from our Buddha Nature is like finding our own well-spring of perfect love and this makes us more self-sufficient.

Also important in developing compassion for ourselves is the ability, and the opportunity, to delight in solitude. Routinely, we spend meaningful time with our loved ones for we know our relationships need this. So why shouldn't we allocate time for the important relationship we have with ourselves? Meditation and mindful living are a chance to make some space for this relationship which in turn strengthens all our relationships.

Love is fair: sharing the domestic load

Children bring massive loads of additional housework and dividing it fairly is a source of tension in most households. We often read reports about the anger and exhaustion of mothers who feel they manage more than their fair share of this load. Many women give up on ever achieving a fair deal, others become eaten up with resentment. Many of us enter a partnership expecting a relationship between equals and end up feeling cheated.

And then there are the partners who—whether due to inflexible workplaces or lack of interest—don't spend enough time with their children and consequently fail to offer us enough of that invaluable child-free time that we so need. Although some partners make valiant attempts to give us our hard-earned breaks, many resent being left alone to look after the children and make sure we leave the house feeling guilty. Although in most households both partners are overstretched by the demands of family life, it's overwhelmingly the woman who receives the shabby end of the deal on issues such as sleep, breaks and housework. We might have far better conditions than our mothers had, but the battle seems far from over.

Many mothers understandably worry that Buddhist teachings, with their emphasis on giving, helping and loving, will turn them into submissive doormats. How can we foster spiritual virtues when we risk being exploited? How can we achieve a fair situation if we don't get angry? How can we love our partners purely when they disregard our feelings about the kind of life we aspire to live? These are difficult questions which many of us agonise over daily, while others, preferring peace of mind, give up.

Recognising the uniqueness of every situation, Buddhism doesn't provide specific solutions on such issues. It requires us to use our judgement. Broadly speaking, all we can do is find loving and skilful ways to resolve our problems. Still, from the Buddhist point of view one thing is sure: anger is not the answer. Although anger is often our habitual response to finding ourselves in an unfair situation, Buddhism would argue that an angry mind does much more damage to ourselves—our happiness, our health, our spiritual progress—that anything we might achieve with it is not worth it.

So where does that leave us? Should we just patiently accept an unjust situation? In Buddhism we don't have to accept bad conditions if we can do something to change them. Consider this oft-quoted verse from the *Guide to the Boddhistva's Way of Life*, by Shantideva:

If something can be remedied,
Why be unhappy about it?
And if there is no remedy for it,
There is still no point in being unhappy.

In short, we do whatever we can and then just be happy. If our partner is way beyond any hope of reform and, for whatever reason, it's impossible to leave him, we practise patient acceptance. Personally, after all those years of feminist struggle by the bold and heroic women that went before me, I'd rather focus on exploring possible remedies. For some the remedy is hiring a cleaner, for some it's rosters and others endless negotiation. To avoid angry confrontations we might consider calm discussions where, after recognising our partner's contribution and even their difficult situation, we ask for more from them. If we feel incapable of calm discussion on this hot potato of a topic, we might consider writing our partner a carefully worded letter, scrupulously prepared.

In any discussion or negotiation with our partner, Buddhist teachings would urge us to take a compassionate approach. It's easy to focus on our own suffering which can so often feel greater than our partner's, but our partner, as a human being, still suffers. It can only help us if we take some time to ponder on the ways in which our partner suffers and to cultivate compassion and concern for them. If this seems like a difficult task, consider the Tibetan officials who, when facing a meeting with the Chinese, work on their feelings of compassion so that their approach can be wholesome. After what the Chinese have done to Tibet, this example can be a great source of inspiration.

Although generosity is an important quality in Buddhism, we still need to use our judgement. A loving family atmosphere is one where each member contributes and nobody feels downtrodden. Accepting what we feel is an unfair share of the load is not loving towards ourselves—giving should always be skilful. To allow family members to grow lazy creates bad karma for them as they condition themselves into habits which become part of their character. Karma—the fact that actions have consequences—not only impacts on our family members but also on the wider society and future generations. If our children learn to see women as domestic servants, this will continue to torment not only our daughters and theirs, but our sons who might perpetuate the inequalities and add to the collective tension between the sexes.

One spiritual friend of mine believes there's a role for patient acceptance in most relationships. Having just finished her thesis on the problems of modern marriage she says:

> We need to take a historical perspective on problems of equality in marriage. We can waste a lot of energy feeling angry that we're at a certain point in history rather than a point further along. It's like saying you want to achieve a doctorate and then feeling really angry that you don't have it right now. As women we can celebrate the enormous progress we've made in the space of a generation and rather than feeling angry, just do all we can to keep moving forward.

There are no neat or perfect answers—as we know, it's very complex. Buddhism doesn't hand us the instructions but gives us some useful guidelines to help us resolve our issues and stop them from spiralling out of control.

Skilful speech

Skilful speech is a category of the Noble Eightfold Path. Interestingly, the Buddha chose not to include it in the category Skilful Action even though speech is undeniably an action. Clearly, he felt it deserved special emphasis and it's easy to understand why. Thinking back, we can see that certain remarks, perhaps made decades ago, can still torment us. The Buddha referred to speech as an axe, a tool of precision and power and a weapon capable of great damage. Of the Ten Evils in Buddhism, three are of the body, three are of the mind and four are of the tongue, and they are lying, slander, abuse and idle talk.

IV. Do not lie, but be truthful. Speak the truth with discretion, fearlessly and in a loving heart.
V. Do not invent evil reports, nor repeat them. Do not find fault, but look for the good sides of your fellow beings, so that you may with sincerity defend them against their enemies.
VI. Do not swear, but speak decently and with dignity.
VII. Do not waste time with gossip, but speak to the purpose or keep silence.

See Appendix 4 for the full list of the Ten Evils.

Skilful speech is invaluable in all areas of our lives but particularly at home. To a greater extent than with any other relationship, our partnership is where we can speak our minds and be ourselves. With our partners it's more acceptable to address problems as they arise, and thankfully so. If we addressed grievances as they arose with our friends, we could find ourselves deserted. The downside of this freedom of expression with our partner, as most of us know only too well, is the potential for conflict.

To use speech skilfully keeps the level of conflict under control. Our style of speech is contagious. When we speak irritably the response is likely to come in the same tone. When your partner offers a cheerful greeting, no matter how you feel, you are likely to find yourself relax a little and respond in a similar way. The way we speak fuels the atmosphere of the house and this may be more important than we realise. A study by Flinders and La Trobe Universities of 750 Australian families (which resonated with similar studies overseas) reported no greater contributor to a well-adjusted adolescent than the social and emotional atmosphere of the house.

Our speech reveals our attitudes and preoccupations and just as we strive to be mindful of these, so we also need to be mindful of our speech and its effects. My husband hears me criticise others, complain about difficulties, rave on about my obsessions and lose my temper. Combing through our conversations it's easy for me to pinpoint areas of spiritual practice that need attention. An interesting exercise practised in some Buddhist schools is 'the 60-second exercise' where two people have a conversation but leave 60 seconds between each response as a way to practise constructive and helpful speech. As mothers we don't have time for such exercises but we might find time to pause briefly before we speak.

So how did the Buddha define skilful speech? First he said it was *truthful*. This suggests the need to be open, frank and simple in our interactions and to avoid lying. Then he said our speech should be *kind* and *gentle*. Refraining from the use of harsh language, we should avoid speech that is malicious, harmful or self-serving. Our speech should be *helpful* too. This means we avoid gossiping, breaking confidences and raving on with no respect for the needs or interests of the listener. One mother explains a change that this teaching brought about for her:

> I realised that I had to stop swearing. If my speech was to be kind, gentle and helpful, I would need to tidy it up. It's not that I was particularly foul-mouthed but certain words are just inflammatory.

She offered some examples:

> I had to stop saying I was 'pissed off', and that someone-or-other didn't 'give a shit'. I had to stop telling my husband about all the 'losers, idiots and morons' I met—how could I ever become compassionate if I used these words. Strong language can have the effect of making you sound angrier than you really are and needlessly escalating tension. And if you can stop thinking in such negative words altogether it's a sound step towards equanimity.

It's also worth keeping in mind the Buddhist principles of:

- **Right person.** Some of us have a tendency to over-communicate when we should turn inwards. If we always take our problems to our partner, or others, we can fail to look for the answers in ourselves; we shut down our own intuition. Others may inundate us with advice, opinions and stories until we stop hearing our inner voice. It's a matter of finding the middle ground, as some of us need to communicate more openly and with more people.
- **Right time and place.** Mark has just shouted at his toddler for accidentally spilling his cereal. Feeling Mark has overreacted to a mere accident, Sharon instantly confronts him. Mark becomes defensive and starts to attack Sharon. They could have avoided the argument entirely if Sharon had allowed Mark's rage to settle and waited for a calmer moment to raise the issue of realistic expectations of toddlers.

  We need to be thoughtful about when to bring up our concerns. It's not always the moment we think of them. If our partner criticises us, it may not be wise to spring to our own defence. If later, after reflection, we feel we were wrongly criticised, we can raise it when the atmosphere is calm and we can do so with a cool head. It helps if we refuse to be provoked into heated argument—issues are rarely resolved at such times. Restraint can be an overlooked virtue.
- **Right subject.** To speak about the right subject we need an awareness of the listener's interests and the intentions behind our words. Before we speak we can pause to ask ourself, 'Why am I saying this? Am I seeking to help, to criticise, to boast, to manipulate, influence, hurt?'

Simple as it sounds, we must remind ourselves to complain less and express appreciation more. This works miracles on the atmosphere of the house. As this mother describes:

> For years I used to wish that my husband would be more appreciative, more affectionate, more willing to tell me something, anything, that he liked about me. Inspired by a good book, I started telling him when he looked handsome, thanking him for his good qualities, giving him more hugs. Maybe I'm just lucky but he actually started returning these small favours. I can't believe it was so simple to put our marriage on a healthier course. The years I wasted!

In summary, before we speak we need to wonder: 'Is what I'm about to say true? Is it kind? Is it beneficial? Could it harm? Is now the time? Should I speak at all?' Asking these questions of ourselves helps us learn from our mistakes, which in my case have been numerous. Mastering skilful speech could take me a long time but at least I can enjoy the benefits of constantly improving.

Some Buddhists find it helps to speak more quietly or slowly, if only to remind themselves to take care. Others make a conscious effort to pause more, purposely inserting a split second before they respond. We don't want to sabotage our joy in conversation with extremes of caution but a commitment to gradual improvement could save us the pain of regret and bad karma.

Listening

To truly listen, to be fully present for another person, is a powerful expression of love. When someone listens to you—quietly, attentively and without judgement—you enjoy a great gift. You have an opportunity to explore your reality, discover ideas, broaden and expand. You can be creative. You find an opportunity to halve your burdens. What a gift the simple act of listening can be within a partnership.

But patient listening doesn't come naturally for most of us. How many people do you know who listen well, who can draw you out and go on your journey? And how does it make you feel when this happens? Restored, liberated, joyous? Listening is a skill, and as with all skills, takes practice and the ability to learn from our failures.

We all want to feel understood and loved for who we are. A commitment to listening allows us to understand our partners more deeply and love each other more sensitively. When we feel our partner hears and understands us, and vice versa, we feel confident we are still of interest to each other. A relationship is on dangerous ground when we stop listening.

Ironically, it's often hardest to listen to those closest to us. With our partners, it was so much easier to listen at the beginning of the relationship when disclosures seemed fresh. We felt inspired and the hormones of new love were doing their work. With time, old habits of half-listening set in: we listen on automatic pilot and perhaps to ourselves more than to what our partners are saying.

Ignoring the truth of impermanence, we now assume we know our partners and what they have to say. Or we let our own expectations, needs and judgements cloud our understanding. To listen well we need to recognise that we never know all there is to know about someone. Everyone we know is changing subtly with each passing day. Listening calls on our imagination, asking that we enter our partner's version of reality.

Opportunities to listen are times of meditation, in that we are relatively silent and we concentrate. Listening is a form of mindfulness as we focus our attention on the other person. We may catch our minds wandering, judging or trying to fix a situation but we return our attention to the speaker's reality. We are mindful of all aspects of their message: the body language, the intonation and most importantly, the underlying feelings behind the words.

To foster the trust that frees people to confide in us we need to surrender control of the conversation. The role of our 'self', our ego, fades into the background as we strive to respond with compassion. We suspend our own judgement just as we do when we meditate: nothing is 'good' or 'bad'. Even if we disagree or disapprove we give the speaker's reality a hearing. We surrender our own agenda along with any need to sound clever or wise. We stop interrupting, commiserating, giving advice and returning the topic to ourselves.

Asking questions is often a way to put ourselves in control of the conversation or to indulge our own curiosity. Let the speaker reveal what they want to. A good way to steer clear of our own agenda is to summarise what people say, or what we perceive them to be feeling. For example, we might respond to their situation saying, 'It sounds really frustrating.' The speaker feels a sense of relief to hear we understand how they feel and is likely to reveal more.

As with skilful speech, we can learn from thinking over our conversations and challenging ourselves, 'To what extent did I listen mindfully? Without judgement? Without offering my opinions and solutions? How focussed was I?' To be skilful listeners, capable of concentration and restraint, ensures we are powerful resources not only to our partners but to our children too. Listening is a reliable path out of selfishness, self-absorption and self-centredness—it makes your world a larger place.

What we can do

- Accept that any relationship and the individuals within it go through seasons, no stage is permanent.
- Dare to initiate improvement with your partner.
- Remember that your children are learning from watching your relationship.
- 'Stop and realise' if you are getting caught in destructive patterns of relating to each other such as bickering, blaming or criticising.
- Check your love for your partner is not attachment, whether it recognises your oneness and whether it includes loving kindness, compassion, sympathetic joy and equanimity.
- Take responsibility for your own role in any relationship difficulties.
- Realise that you can choose your responses, they are not the inevitable result of your situation.
- Consider your partner's point of view often and encourage them to do likewise.
- Recognise the importance of compassion for yourself—remind yourself of your own acts of kindness and your Buddha Nature.
- Make time to work on your relationship with yourself. Delight in solitude.

- Sort out the allocation of domestic labour in a skilful way rather than with overt conflict and avoid accepting a deal which oppresses yourself and encourages family members to be irresponsible.
- Realise that your mode of speech is contagious.
- Comb through conversations with your partner as a way to pinpoint areas for spiritual attention.
- Pause before you speak.
- Endeavour to keep your speech truthful, kind, gentle and helpful.
- Speak to the right person—sometimes this is yourself.
- Learn the value of restraint and postponement.
- Speak with regard for your listener's needs and interests.
- Consider expressing more appreciation and fewer complaints to your partner.
- Take time to listen to your partner without judging, interrupting, or steering the conversation.

CHAPTER 8

finding happiness *and* losing our self-image

Oh the hours I've spent philosophising about happiness. How do we find it? How do we keep it? Is a feeling of complete happiness even possible? So often any happiness we experience is tinged with anxiety: how can we hold onto this? Do we even deserve this? Do we have any right to be happy when so many live in sorrow?

Many have made fortunes from marketing their 'ten secrets for happiness'. Is there a secret to happiness? One memorable evening, a Buddhist teacher explained what struck me as the first secret of happiness. It was a moment of realisation which saw me intensify my commitment to practising Buddhism. I felt like she'd handed me the first piece in the happiness puzzle. She said: 'Any happiness we glean from the world outside us is only temporary. Deep and lasting happiness needs to come from within.'

Reflecting over the moments of peace and happiness in my life I found this to be true. Happiness from external sources did tend to be temporary and even tinged with anxiety. When my baby Zac was first plonked on my tummy I had never known such joy, but soon came the doubts and worries. Will he survive? Will someone steal him? Could I be a good enough mother? And in no time this source of happiness was screaming for hours every evening making me as distraught as I'd ever been.

Where we don't find happiness

'Happiness comes from within' can seem like a tired old cliché. We've all heard it before but even if we agree, consider how much time we spend seeking happiness from the outside world rather than within ourselves. For some reason, we always seek happiness from outer sources, incapable of believing the truth that happiness is available to us in any moment.

Our lives are rife with desires, expectations and outright demands on the world. We tell ourselves the world must provide a loving partner, children that make us proud, friends that adore us, a satisfying career, masses of possessions, regular excitement and that's only the beginning of our demands. If we find unsatisfactoriness in one area we focus on it and empower it to make us unhappy. If we're fortunate in one of these areas we may experience great happiness—but it doesn't last.

Even if life were meeting our expectations we'd raise the bar and decide that we must need more. Now that we have acquired the comfortable home, we may as well go for the magnificent home—then we can be happy, then we'll know peace once and for all.

If-only syndrome

We keep deluding ourselves that happiness is just round the corner, but always in the future. 'If I could just get out of school', becomes, 'If I could only find a better job', which becomes, 'If I could just find someone to love', and so on, potentially for the rest of our lives. How many of us said, 'If only I could have children, then I'd be happy'? We soon found that children brought us great joy but also countless hurdles and miseries. With happiness always round the next corner, we could come to the end of our lives to find that we never allowed ourselves to be happy in the present moment and that we therefore wasted countless opportunities to experience joy.

We ceaselessly categorise our experiences into 'good' or 'bad'. Then we try to arrange our lives so that we can avoid the 'bad' and attract the 'good'. Despite these efforts we live in failure. As any Zen Buddhist will tell you: life presents 'ten thousand joys and ten thousand sorrows'. We must meet pain as well as pleasure, so we can't afford to hook our happiness to external circumstances.

In our clearer moments we may glimpse what's going on—this endless pursuit of transitory happiness seems futile but what can we do? Rather than acknowledge the inner deprivation we try harder in the outer world because we obviously need more of what it can offer. We might convince ourselves we need a world trip, an affair or an exciting career change. And we're back in the cycle of demanding from the outside world.

We run about in a frenzy and may manage to distract ourselves from our inner world, but eventually, we feel the need to make some time to stop doing and simply be. As Buddhist writer Sylvia Boorstein called one of her books: *Don't Just Do Something, Sit There.* Meditation and mindful living reconnect us with our inner selves. If we learn to seek our happiness from within instead of linking it to external circumstances, we'll find strength to face the challenges life hurls at us. The challenge is to stop looking outside ourselves for happiness. We need to start an inner journey.

Happiness, or the lack of it, can be an issue that mothers feel desperate to resolve. This is especially the case on the arrival of a second child. Parenting magazine *Sydney's Child* reported the results of a study which found: '. . . a woman's life satisfaction falls to its all-time low the year after the birth of her second child. Another study found that many second-time mothers had stress levels high enough to warrant medical treatment.'

Mothers spend so much time attending to the 'have-to's of life: housework, errands, paper work, phone calls, taxiing, appointments, birthdays. We need to give all our family members quality time and maintain contact with a string of relatives. Our brains are shuffling so many details that they feel close to exploding.

With family responsibilities we are far less free to seek our own happiness. We have less time for our careers, hobbies and friends and we may discover that a 'family holiday' is a contradiction in terms. At times any hope of happiness for a mother is quashed by a baby's bellowing, a toddler's tantrum, a daughter's sleep problems, a son's anti-social behaviour or workplace inflexibility. There's no end to the hoops our children and others can put us through. At times happiness is the most distant of our dreams and we humbly confine our wishes to 'a little peace and quiet'.

Certainly a mother has new sources of happiness from the world outside her: watching her children grow into little characters, laughing at their capers, perhaps a new circle of friends. Still, she may find herself in the cycle of postponing happiness, wishing,

'If I could just have them all at school', 'If we could only get through this stage', 'If they would just move out!'

We sometimes catch more experienced mothers musing: 'They grow up so quickly, don't they?' Some of us don't believe them but still, this period of our lives will pass and this makes it precious. Buddhist writer and mother Anne Cushman understands this:

> Could there be any better way to get my nose rubbed in the truth of impermanence than to love a child in a jagged, careless world? . . . And even if everything goes absolutely perfectly, I know that this particular Skye—the one who warbles and passionately sucks on the bill of his rubber duck as he splashes with me in the tub—is going to dissolve like bubble bath. Yesterday he was a kicking bulge in my belly as I swam laps in the July sun; tomorrow he'll be a middle-aged man, weeping and scattering my ashes in a mountain lake.

See Appendix 5 for her account of mothering a newborn from a Buddhist perspective.

In postponing our happiness until the children are older, we lose sight of the importance of this stage of our lives. When we're older, perhaps as we leaf through a photo album brimming with images from their childhood, we might regret that we never allowed ourselves to enjoy our small children as much as we could have. The studies keep finding that the first few years of life are the most important to a child's psychological and intellectual development—another reminder of the preciousness of our moments with young children.

The self-image quandary

Before we had children we could arrange our lives to include activities that nourished our self-image. If we didn't have satisfying careers we could always pursue other interests in our search for fulfilment and a sense of identity. We were young and felt as though we always would be. Although we were never completely trouble-free, life was a lighter experience offering myriad distractions from the problems of the world. It was easier to hide from that first Noble Truth, that there is suffering and unsatisfactoriness—aging, sickness and death were the last things on our minds.

Now we find ourselves with children. Many of us have wound down our careers and it's hard to find time to indulge in interests outside work and family. We might find ourselves questioning, 'Who am I?', and feel like we don't know anymore. How do we piece together a self-image now? Although there are exceptions, those wonderful born-to-mother types, most of us find responding to the demands of our children all day long does little to bolster our self-image. A friend informed her demanding three-year-old daughter, 'I'm not your slave!' only to be assured, 'Yes you are!'

There are times when we feel proud to call ourselves mothers, when we feel like we've 'got it all'. But sometimes our self-image comes under severe attack as our child-rearing problems overwhelm us or we see our lifestyle as one of unrelenting sacrifice. We've all heard mothers lament: 'I get so little time to myself and when I do I'm so exhausted I can't use it', 'My career is finished', 'All I do is respond to the needs of others' and, at worst, 'I don't know who I am anymore'. All symptoms of a self-image under siege.

As my Buddhist friend Joanne put it:

> In the months after my second child was born, as I felt the self I once knew recede beyond recalling, I thought perhaps this is what going mad must feel like. And in the months that followed I watched helplessly as the perfect mother in me died a quick and horrible death.

How can a mother foster a positive self-image in a day filled with activities that stimulate children, a day filled with chores, appointments and errands? Many seek the answer in work, but how reliable a source of self-image are our jobs? We may be in a job that does more to damage our self-image than prop it up. Or our working conditions could change overnight and the sources of our self-image dry up. Moreover, the juggle of kids and work may lead us to feel like we do neither job well.

What does Buddhism have to say on the issue? It takes two words to sum up the Buddhist position on self-image: DROP IT. In fact, Buddhism goes as far as saying that your self-image, your insistence that you exist in some kind of stable, consistent and permanent form, is making you miserable.

The pursuit of identity

Our craving for an identity is a burden. We feel that we can only be happy if we are 'worthy' and 'valuable'. We compile mental lists of our good points and bad points and constantly monitor our performance. We demand that we be different from how we see ourselves now. Not many people would want to admit that their aim in life is to create a positive self-image, it's like saying, 'I invest most of my energy in trying to feel really proud of myself.' Although this doesn't sound very admirable, if we look at many of our thoughts and behaviours, this is what they reveal. It's possible we devote most of our lives to fulfilling the craving for a positive self-image.

How often do we find ourselves:

- striving to be the perfect mother, worker, homemaker—no matter what the cost to our health and sanity?
- feeling guilty when we don't meet our expectations?
- comparing ourselves with others?
- worrying about others' opinions of us?
- overreacting at even the hint of criticism?
- seeking others' approval?

It could be on our deathbeds that we finally realise: I spent my whole life searching for self-esteem—there must have been a better way to live. The Buddhist perspective would be: why bother chasing a positive self-image when you don't even have a 'self'? That is to say there is no essential You in any stable, consistent or ongoing way. The teaching of *no-self* may at first seem outrageous but after you investigate it you may be surprised at how much it rings true.

Who are you anyway?

If it were possible to write down the script of your thoughts, would it read like the monologue of one actor? Or would it be more like reading a script for several actors each with a distinct agenda? Consider this mother's train of thought:

> Maybe I should call Anne for a chat . . . she's probably a bit lonely on her own . . . I've just got so much to do though, I don't really have time . . . she's always been a good friend to me though and I should be more caring . . . I don't really feel that chatty actually, I'm a bit tired . . . I must call the accountant.

It's as if our minds contain several personalities: there's the voice that makes suggestions, the voice that vetoes action, the voice that forces you to consider others' feelings—there's a whole committee of personalities competing for dominance. These competing voices may plunge you into confusion and indecision or you may obey the loudest one and deal with the others later.

Which voice is your self? All the voices exist in your own head yet they all seem to have different personalities. Listening to the chatter that takes place in our minds, do we find one voice that we could consider as consistent over time? Could it be that our tendency to see our self as one coherent entity is a delusion?

The search for a self

Buddhism challenges us: how rational is it to believe in an ongoing, stable self at all? For starters, how would you define the self? What exactly is it? Would you use descriptive labels? 'I am impatient and pessimistic but also affectionate and sociable.' To describe ourselves with these labels assumes that we have personality traits that don't change over time. Yet our tendency to be impatient, affectionate or any other quality varies from one day to the next. None of these qualities is locked in for life.

Perhaps we could define our self as the result of our past experiences? But that puts us at the mercy of memory which is notoriously unreliable. It's human nature to fiddle with our past: some memories we suppress, others we relive many times distorting them in the process. We edit our memories, embellish them and create convenient details that might never have existed. Besides, if faced with the same events a few years later we might behave completely differently and create entirely different stories. Even if we had perfect memories, our past experiences don't define us. We may have been victimised at school but it's our choice whether we *identify* with such experiences and become card-carrying victims for the rest of our lives.

So, could we define our self as the roles we play? When we go to social functions, people ask us, 'What do you do?' to get some insight into who we are. Yet what we do hardly provides a complete picture, especially if we don't like our job. Neither could we define our self by the roles 'loving partner', 'loyal daughter' or 'competent mother'. Our capacity or desire to play any of these roles day in and day out over time varies enormously.

We have a body which appears to be separate from others and the rest of the world. But could we see this body as being a stable, consistent self? The changes that our bodies undergo from birth to death, along with the fact that we shed and renew cells all the time, certainly suggest that the body is no place to look for a permanent unchanging self.

A new meditator decides to concentrate on their breath only to find that a dozen different voices from their own mind interrupt them. Thoughts run off in ever-changing and confusing directions. They are surprised to find that their 'self' is not in control here, just as when they sleep they, or their self, can neither control nor remember their dreams.

The possible sources of our sense of self are plentiful. Which ones should we choose? We may look to other people to define our self and feel devastated when they don't like us. Sometimes we feel our self is what we see in the mirror: if we *look* less than attractive, then we feel less worthwhile, less valuable. Maybe we are what we eat, or what we have written in our diaries, or how we behaved yesterday. Are we our résumés or are we the images in our photo albums? None of these and all of these. The more we speculate the more complex it becomes to find a way to define self.

The findings

So we find that coming up with a water-tight definition of our self is impossible. We are, in fact, a collection of bits and pieces that do not fit together in any logical way, that contradict each other and change constantly. You, your self, cannot be found and therefore cannot be relied on for a sense of stability. Rather than being a stable object, the self is a collection of interactive processes, constantly transforming, a set of verbs rather than nouns or adjectives. Any sense of self we may have is an invention, as the Buddha realised as he sat under his tree:

> *The being which I believed in was a fictional construction! I have a name, a personal history, memories, thoughts, emotions, dreams; but when I look they are quite illusory.*

The message here seems to be that we are not who we think we are, that we have no idea of who we really are. We simply don't exist in the way we think we do.

Despite the lack of conclusive evidence for a self, we act in ways that protect our fragile ego, constantly seeing the world in terms of 'I', 'my' and 'mine'. Buddhism teaches us that this quest for a self makes us miserable—let it go. Yet it is such a habit, so automatic, that it's difficult to give up.

Many Buddhists believe the teaching of *no-self* should be taught with great caution, presented at the level of understanding of the listener, in case we misunderstand. For example, we might believe we don't exist or don't matter, and therefore that nothing could matter. In this way Buddhism might be misinterpreted as promoting indifference and withdrawal from life, which is not the message of the Buddha at all. The teaching is complex and counter-intuitive and we each need to explore it further for ourselves.

The good news on no-self

Part of us feels threatened by the concept of *no-self*, believing that it undermines all our striving to become 'the person we are today'. Having a self is familiar territory—we are used to thinking in this way and it would take a revolution of the mind to dispense with the notion.

Another part of us may respond to this teaching with relief: finally we can give up our tortuous efforts to define ourselves, to protect and defend our contrived self-images. Who needs a precious self-image anyway? Now we can identify and do away with all our restrictive self-definitions. 'I hate parties', for example, 'I say what people expect me to say', 'I avoid risk', 'I must visit my relatives', 'I mustn't waste money'. All the rules that we've used in the past, and that serve to restrict our behaviour, become irrelevant. Understanding that we have a true nature, our Buddha Nature, behind our false perception of who we are, is to walk out of our cage.

At first the idea of having no self could be disconcerting—is there any need to behave, to act responsibly if there is no self to govern behaviour?—but Buddhism teaches that in shedding the delusion of a self we uncover our true nature, our Buddha Nature, which is one of wisdom and compassion. This then allows us to ask, 'What does this moment require?' rather than 'How do *I* respond to such moments?' and to meet each new moment with a freshness, a beginner's mind free of prejudice. As mothers this is what we do when we are at our best, as Susan Murphy explains:

> Parenting will call into question virtually everything we think we know, beginning with who we think we are. (We're not!) Children have an extraordinary talent for breaking apart our roles, demanding again and again that we meet them right in the moment, meet our lives, meet difficulty, moment by moment meet and resolve the extraordinary mystery of 'the other'. To do this we must time and again lose our precious adult facades and have recall or regain access to the mysterious and creative core that has no name, the source, that we brush again and again in meditation.

The delusion that we are independent, or separate and cut off from others and all that is 'outside me', also arises from this false notion of self. Our attachment to an ego disconnects us from those around us and we overlook the reality that we are all one, a connected, interdependent whole. And importantly, our false perception of a separate self is the main obstacle in cultivating the Buddhist 'mind of love'. When our life is focussed on ourself and what's ours, we are blocked from seeing the needs of others. We fall prone to using others as report cards on how likeable or powerful we are, or on how many people love us. We treat others according to what they do for us or how they make us feel. Ironically, the self-oriented approach does not make us happy.

Our obsession with a self may hinder us from truly listening to others. When we are self-conscious, self-absorbed or seeking self-esteem we miss many chances to talk with others in meaningful and helpful ways. We may overlook opportunities to help others even when helping them might not take much effort. It's hardly any trouble to mind our friend's child when she needs some time to herself, but caught up with our own concerns we don't think to offer. It takes no effort to offer reassurance to a suffering relation, but, absorbed in self, we turn the conversation topic to our own experience: 'That's just like me, I . . .'

The problem now is that we've grown so conditioned to carting this 'self' around that it takes time and great effort to dispense with it. Even if we have come to an intellectual understanding of the concept of *no-self*, living this is another matter. At a surface level we may understand how our sense of self sabotages us, but we must achieve insight on a deep level before we can experience the full power of this teaching. This can only happen through meditation and the mindfulness that it brings.

Mirror, mirror, don't do this to me!

For women, no discussion on self-image would be complete without a reference to the image that stares back at us from our mirrors. The shallow consumer culture that we live in does its utmost to tell us that who we are, our self, and our worth, is what we look like. High school culture reinforces this for most of us and even now it's very rare to meet a woman who has learned to accept the way she looks, let alone the fact that she's ageing. And nothing speeds up the ageing process like having children. If we didn't put on weight during our pregnancies or time spent at home feeding infants, most of us at least have some deepened wrinkles testifying to how much sleep we lost.

My friend Rachel, who occasionally emails me her articles, agonises about her physical decline:

> I'm aging. Not drastically, but at 35 I don't exactly look youthful and with the decay ahead I need to find a way to get used to it. I've had the babies and the sleepless nights babies bring and now it's written all over my face and body.

> What's really bothering me is how much time I agonise over my appearance. With a toddler and a baby who won't grant me leave to develop my mind I have managed to find time to frown into the mirror (although you generally should avoid frowning as it only deepens wrinkles). When you're not glowering at the mirror, you're gazing into the perfect faces of children, coveting their flawless skin and soft hair.
>
> My mind once abounded with worthy thoughts. Now I find myself thinking about open pores, thinning hair and crow's feet not to mention my complete failure at abdominal reform. Last night my husband told me that I needed support—he didn't mean emotional.
>
> I am cursed with a catwalk-gorgeous sister. She got married recently and her wedding was a celebration of female beauty. After looking through two-thousand-and-five-zillion wedding photos where I, the bridesmaid, looked like some demented cousin I knew I hadn't been worrying about my appearance for nothing. I panicked and started consulting plastic surgeons with my 13 suggestions for procedures. I even went through with one procedure. Although nobody has spotted the change, I can see an improvement.

As with all life's problems, ageing gives us an opportunity to deepen our wisdom. As our youth slips away Buddhist teachings can help us.

Facing ageing

As Rachel's case illustrates, we resist the inevitable process of change in our bodies. It's not that it's wrong to keep fit, buy eye creams or even undergo plastic surgery. According to Buddhism, the problems start when we develop feelings of attachment to the ideas of youth and beauty, when we chase them graspingly and believe they could make us happy in any lasting way. The attachment, according to the second Noble Truth, is what makes us suffer. We may even be capable of seeing how our attachment makes us suffer yet still refuse to give it up. We may see that our attachment damages our relationships with others, just as Rachel is aware of her jealousy for her sister.

So many of our attachments or desires are based on the delusion of having a self. Rachel craves youth and beauty to feed her self-esteem, even though the endless pursuit of self-esteem is hardly the road to happiness. She deludes herself that she'll feel some peace if she can reform her abdomen. But she must know deep down that this is unlikely to be the case. A 'washboard stomach' would allow her to feel some relief that she no longer has this desire but the feeling of relief would fade, and she'd focus on her double chin or her thighs.

Examining our anxiety about ageing reveals a Buddhist truth about all unhappiness and suffering: It is not always the suffering itself that makes us miserable so much as our resistance to it.

Love handles and furrowed foreheads don't actually hurt us. In some cultures they would even deliver us status and respect. It's our aversion to ageing that makes us miserable: the energy we invest in avoiding it, the time we spend fearing it. It's the way we tell ourselves that if we could only get rid of our crow's feet we'd feel so much better; it's the way we feel self-conscious with others—certain that they're examining our decay.

We choose for ourselves how painful the experience of ageing will be. Are we going to resist the inevitable? Panic? Grieve? Become gloomy? Or will we do what we can to look our best and then get on with our lives? As the Buddhist author Sylvia Boorstein so wisely states: 'Suffering is inevitable; pain is optional.'

This is not to say that we need to deny or suppress our true feelings about ageing. If aging is a painful experience then we need to explore those feelings and get to the root of them. What beliefs do we cherish on the subject and how rational are they? Is the issue really how we look or are there deeper issues to deal with such as loneliness, the need for control over the uncontrollable or just a painful sense of inadequacy. As any Buddhist teacher will tell us, acceptance is the only approach to a process—ageing—over which we ultimately hold little control.

Facing death

Resisting ageing is like resisting death. Morbid as it sounds, they're both going to catch us so why live in denial? Living in awareness of the certainty of ageing and death is a priority for Buddhists. It's a way of embracing the concept of impermanence. Some women become suddenly and painfully aware of their own mortality through the experience of motherhood. As my Buddhist friend Joanne describes:

> The agony of my labour experience made me face for the first time that I will die one day and it terrified me because I couldn't bear the thought of leaving my child without a mother. I felt a renewed need to take care of myself. But my awareness of mortality was heightened further by the vulnerability of the newborn. Feeling blessed with abundance only increased my terror. I was very aware that this baby would, some day, die. I had given birth to a being with a finite life. These realisations were very hard-hitting for me.

In our culture, it is seen as bizarre to dwell on moribund thoughts: death makes us feel uncomfortable so we avoid reflecting on it. But given death is the only certainty in life, maybe it's worth more attention. If we allowed our mind to dwell for a while on what it would be like to lose the use of one leg, it would make us appreciate having two. If we forced ourselves to reflect on sickness for a few moments, it would make us appreciate our good health. In the same way, if we regularly consider the certainty of our own death, we learn to appreciate life. With death in mind, we are likely to use our lives more thoughtfully.

Most of us have heard of people who, after a near-death experience, realised how precious their lives were and made dramatic changes. They stopped taking life for granted and decided to use their time more productively. They realised what matters and what is mere froth.

To remind themselves of the certainty of death, some Buddhists make their first thought on waking: 'Wow! I made it through the night without dying.' Some recite a mantra: 'birth, ageing, pain and death'. Others meditate on the degeneration of their bodies or on death itself. They envision their bodies buried in the ground and picture the skin slowly rotting, the bones gradually disappearing. All these practices make it easier to remember our impermanence. I'm not sure if women's magazines will ever embrace such ideas, but maybe a more realistic and accepting approach to death could help us cope with the inevitability of ageing.

Insight

When I was a teenager with frizzy hair and pimples, my mother, after assuring me I was beautiful, pointed out that if you look at the people at the train station, in the bank queue, on the street, only a tiny proportion of them are 'beautiful' in any commercial sense. My own surveys found her to be right and yet these 'plain' members of the public probably belong to loving families. Some of them have stimulating careers, others hobbies that make their hearts sing. If pressed, Rachel would probably admit that ordinary-looking people can find what they aspire to and that youth and beauty are not the way to everlasting peace and happiness. She might remember the high rate of despair and self-destructive behaviour exhibited by the world's beautiful celebrities. She might acknowledge some of the problems that beauty brings, such as envy and being loved not for who you are but how you look.

Insight, or the ability to see *what is*, helps us to see when our thoughts and actions are out of sync with what we know to be true.

Although we can see a truth plainly with our intellect, such as 'beauty doesn't bring happiness', we often act in a way that suggests we don't understand the truth at all. We need to pay close attention to our thoughts so that we can identify these mismatches between what we know to be true and how we live. Of equal importance is the need to pay attention to the beliefs and assumptions we cling to, for these are often the cause of our problems.

For example, on reflection, Rachel might uncover the assumptions: 'Beauty will bring me peace', 'If I pay enough I can avoid ageing' and 'With a disciplined beauty regime I can stay young'. She might identify the demands she makes on life: 'To be worthwhile, I have to look good', 'My husband must find me attractive and tell me so' and 'Expensive beauty treatments must work'.

Take diets—the world of dieting is an excellent example of how we ignore the underlying issues. We know diets don't work and that all we lose is some faith in ourselves. We become so obsessed with our dream body shape that we have no idea of the answers to the more important underlying questions:

- Why do I feel inadequate in the first place?
- Would my unpleasant feelings be forever resolved by mere slimness? How rational is it to base my self-acceptance on a body shape?
- What thoughts trigger my overeating?
- Why does my body feel uncomfortable and can eating fix it?

If Rachel could explore her unspoken assumptions and demands, she might find that they, not her appearance, are the cause of her dissatisfaction.

Most Buddhist traditions argue that *thinking* our way to insight with our scatty, unreliable thought processes will not always be effective. It's thinking that plunges us into our mental messes so it might not be the best tool for cleaning them up. The most effective path to insight, they argue, is to use the clear-mindedness of meditation where you can transcend the rational, thinking mind and see your thoughts for what they are. When we see our delusions clearly, our misconceptions and bad habits disappear effortlessly. If this doesn't happen, or if our delusions resurface, it only means we haven't seen our misconceptions clearly enough.

To pay attention to our thoughts as they arise is exceedingly difficult, especially for beginners. Anyone who has tried meditating knows that we all suffer from 'monkey minds' that jump around and seem to live a chaotic life of their own, well beyond our control. To increase our attention span takes discipline and patient hours of meditation. As we practise meditation over time, our minds become clearer and more disciplined so we can achieve the insights that can transform our experiences and hence our lives.

What we can do

- Realise that deep and lasting happiness can only come from within—stop relying on the world outside you to deliver.
- Stop postponing happiness and enjoy your present moment.
- Make time to stop doing and just 'be'. For example, meditate.
- Realise that slavishly attending to a positive self-image does not lead to happiness.
- Don't get locked into any particular image of your self. According to Buddhism, your perception of your self is an invention.
- You can only reach true understanding of the teaching of no-self through meditation—it is a matter of insight or deep realisation rather than intellectual understanding.
- Attachment to youth and beauty causes suffering, as ageing and death are inevitable. Work on letting go, on acceptance.
- Realise ageing doesn't hurt you, only your resistance to it.
- Take time to dwell on the only certainty in your life: death. It helps you to live more consciously.

Chapter 9

meditating

WHY WOULD A MOTHER, with all the competing demands for her time, make time to meditate? There would have to be some very compelling reasons. And there are. In Chapter 2 we saw how mindfulness—which we practise in meditation—provides us with *energy* to fulfil our daily tasks, *calm* to deal with negative emotions and *insights* which help us learn and grow spiritually. Mindfulness helps us to be attentive parents who are more capable of seeing our situations clearly. We've also seen that the more we can live in the present, as practised in meditation, the more fully we live our lives and the more joy we find.

As the Buddha said, with our minds we create our world. The more healthy, positive and kind our minds are, the more happiness we can experience and the more benefits for our children. Buddhism teaches that meditation is the best tool for transforming our minds. Meditation is a time to become familiar with more positive mind states, to immerse ourselves in them and to experience for ourselves a taste of clarity, calmness and kindness. In meditation we rehearse a higher way of being which we gradually transfer to our day-to-day life.

A wealth of medical findings pointing to the positive effects of meditation on our health have also been documented. Dr Herbert Benson, a Harvard Medical School professor, studied the impact of meditation for almost 30 years and found meditators decreased their visits to health professionals by more than a third. He claims that when the body is in a state of deep calm it repairs itself. Whereas stress interferes with our body's state of balance, making us less immune to disease and infection, deep relaxation puts our bodies into a state of balance conducive to healing.

Dr Benson is by no means alone. Other medical researchers report that the calm we find in meditation eases our stress levels throughout the day, lowers our blood pressure by up to 50 per cent and improves our heart function. Meditation has also been proven to help us sleep more soundly and improve our general mood. A survey by the American Association of Health Plans found that eight out of ten doctors think meditation should be included in their training for the sake of both doctors and patients. It's becoming a cliché to say that if meditation came in a pill, we'd pay a fortune for it.

The benefits of a meditating mother to family life are also clear. When I ask mothers why they meditate they say: 'It makes me calmer', 'I have less trouble with anger', 'It helps me keep annoyances in perspective', 'I feel happier/less confused/less crabby and irritable'. As this mother said:

> I meditate as a form of anger-management, anxiety-management and general negativity management. But it's not just about dealing with the negatives, it's also a way to connect with the positive and create potential for joy and happiness and a whole new way of seeing my life.

Chittaprabha is an ordained member of the Friends of the Western Buddhist Order. With her long blond hair and energetic ways she appears younger than me, even though she is now a grandmother of five. Chittaprabha makes some interesting points about the benefits of meditation:

> Too much task-oriented activity can remove us from the essential experience of being fully present and from seeing and responding to the beauty and suffering around us. Through meditation I discover a spaciousness of mind which allows a deeper sense of my relationship to the world and a deeper intimacy and confidence in myself. My perspective broadens and instead of operating through the power mode I interact through the love mode. I have found ways of sharing this sense of spaciousness with children, sometimes through appreciation of nature and being kind to animals.
>
> Through meditation and increased awareness. I learn that life goes far beyond my own immediate needs and

> circumstances. I touch a much deeper intuition of the interconnectedness of life. Importantly, I start to realise the consequences of my actions, and this has led to a more refined ethical sense.

Given these benefits, meditation might turn out to be one of the greatest discoveries of our life. Of course, as with any new skill, we struggle at first—we face doubts and allow ourselves to be tempted by all the other activities we could be doing. But with the potential of meditation to improve every aspect of our lives—emotional, physical, spiritual, psychological—we may become committed to it sooner than we expected.

There are many different meditation techniques in Buddhism and you may eventually choose one that most helps you with your specific situation and your specific character tendencies. In this chapter we investigate the two most common forms of Buddhist meditation: mindfulness of the breath meditation and loving kindness meditation. Bear in mind though, all Buddhist traditions emphasise the importance of learning meditation directly from a qualified teacher.

First things first

Buddhist teachers often recommend establishing a special place set aside for meditating. Some meditators delight in decorating this spot with meaningful symbols: a picture of the Buddha, a statue, some incense, candles, photos of your teacher or other inspiring Buddhists, some verses from the scriptures. You could build your own altar. If you can create a space with atmosphere, you make your practice more alluring, but this is optional. My husband wants no such space in his house—the poor love finds it all 'too weird' so I make do without. It's enough for him to have a wife who likes to 'sit in a trance', let alone live with all the strange paraphernalia, so I won't push it.

Traditionally, meditators sit cross-legged on the floor but a straight-backed chair does the job. What's important is to keep your posture upright—slouching and slumping leads to aches and sleepiness. Short of time for formal sittings, you might be tempted to meditate in bed on waking. It's a poor substitute for a formal sitting and makes it harder to reach an adequate level of concentration. Still, some days it's all the time you will find and trying to meditate is better than lying there in a state of dread about the day ahead. Like any time of the day, it's another opportunity to practise mindfulness. No matter what your position, try to meditate with your eyes the slightest bit open. It may feel awkward at first but allowing a little light in wards off sleepiness.

If possible your meditation should take place when you wake in the morning because your mind is relatively clutter-free. Still, the best time to meditate is always personal. Some people feel too groggy in the morning and find meditating before bedtime ensures a restful night. Others find evening sittings make them too alert or give them too much energy to fall asleep. To prepare your mind for meditation a calming activity may help—yoga, reading spiritual writings, ironing, folding laundry or anything that helps you slow down and focus.

Although the types of meditation that Buddhists use are many, there is one common to all schools and invariably it is the first one we learn when new to Buddhism. Usually called 'mindfulness of breath', it requires that we sit still, relax, close our eyes and be aware of the rise and fall of our breath. We don't need to *think* about the breath or control it in any way. Neither do we need to concentrate really, really hard. It's more a case of relaxing and watching our breath as you eventually become one with its rise and fall. When our attention wanders, we patiently bring it back to our breath without any mental comment.

A new meditator finds focussing their attention impossible, so the meditation often includes some built-in support. Many meditators find it helps to bring their attention to the breath by easing slowly into the first stage. My meditation teacher gradually lowers the class into mindfulness of breath by focussing on relaxing first. Slowly, she guides:

> Close your eyes and listen to all the sounds . . . bring your attention to the room and the people in it . . . and now consider your own body: it's shape, the points where it connects with the floor . . . gradually work your attention down your body releasing any tension you find, starting with the scalp . . . now focussing on your facial muscles, allow your face to feel like soft, melting butter . . . and moving down to your neck . . .

After moving down the whole body, we start to watch the rise and fall of each breath.

Counting each breath, as a way to anchor your attention, can also help. One approach is the four-stage meditation described below and taught by the Friends of the Western Buddhist Order in their introductory courses. On days when you feel focussed and clear you might concentrate on your breath without using the four stages—you can always come back to them if you find your mind wandering too often. Roughly five minutes on each stage is the general advice for beginners, but don't be too concerned with clock-watching. Those new to meditation who find it difficult might want to start with only a few minutes and gradually increase the time with each sitting.

Mindfulness of breath meditation

1. When we first bring our attention to our breath we count each breath on the **out-breath**. We count from one to ten over and over again. The counting helps us control our attention but our focus is on the breath, not the numbers.

2. In the second stage, we continue counting the breaths but we count on the **in-breath**, rather than the out-breath. The difference from stage one is only slight but the shift causes a subtle deepening of concentration.

3. In the third stage, we do away with the anchor of counting and start to focus on the **whole breathing process** and any sensations it triggers. We might notice the stillness between the breaths, the rise and fall of the abdomen or the sound of our breathing.

4. In the fourth stage, we refine the process by **fixing our attention** on one aspect of breathing. We feel the sensation of the breath on the point where it leaves and enters our bodies—that is, round about the nostrils or the **tip of the nose**. We may notice for example how the air we take in is slightly cooler than the air we breathe out.

   We wind up the fourth stage by returning our awareness to the general breathing process again and then to the sensations of the body. Gradually, we bring the meditation to a close and open our eyes. Alternatively, we can sit with ourselves mindfully and enjoy the stillness. This could be a time to just watch what happens, see what comes up, be.

When we have finished meditating and return to the demands of our day, we strive to hold onto the mindfulness and stillness we achieved during meditation for as long as we can. With determination we strive to keep our mind in the present moment throughout our day, paying close attention to whatever is before us or within us. As with the meditation session, when we become distracted by thoughts of the past and future, we bring our mind back to the moment with patience, persistence and gentleness.

Skilful Effort

I remember when I first learned this four-stage meditation the teacher warned us that we might find ourselves losing count of our breaths reaching, say, 17, before catching ourselves. I thought, 'How could you get all the way to 17 without realising it?' The very next week, I found myself at 45—I must have been sleepy.

The truth of the matter is that your mind *will* wander. This is normal and you don't need to become frustrated or self-recriminatory. The three buzzwords are: patience, persistence and gentleness. If you find yourself tensing up or frowning with the effort to rein in your concentration, then you're trying too hard. The aim is to watch the breath without mental struggle. In terms of the Noble Eightfold Path, we need to achieve Skilful Effort in our meditation. This means walking the middle ground between intensity and sleepiness, between strain and languor.

ACHIEVING INSIGHT DURING MEDITATION

In the four-stage meditation we deal with distractions by returning our attention to the breath. Yet meditation has even greater potential if we allow our distractions to run their course but observe them mindfully. This is far more difficult, especially for those new to meditation who might struggle to concentrate. The ability to watch our thoughts mindfully without allowing ourselves to become entangled in them could be a longer-term goal to pursue when our concentration has improved. Certainly, the ability to observe our own thoughts helps us achieve life-changing insights and dispense with our more self-defeating beliefs and behaviours.

Whether we watch our distractions or resist them, we don't approach meditation specifically seeking insight—we merely provide the conditions for insight to arise by striving to make our minds clear. Helen Jandamit is a mother and meditation teacher with a flair for analogies. She explains how meditation paves the way for insight: 'Watching the breath gradually becomes like a white background. If a speck of dust is placed on a white background, it is easier to see its form than if it is placed on a dusty surface.'

With practice and a deepening of concentration the speck and all its attributes become clearer still. And when we see our deepest tendencies for what they really are, they lose their power to control us. Insight is what makes us understand what's really going on in our life so that we can become aware of, and change, our habitual reactions and behaviour.

Insight also gives us a chance to understand the Buddha's teachings not just intellectually but through direct experience, a far more powerful agent of change. In *Handbook for Mankind*, Buddhadasa Bhikkhu lists some of the teachings that insight can illuminate for us:

> The expression 'insight into the true nature of things' refers to seeing transience, unsatisfactoriness and non-selfhood; seeing that no thing is worth getting, no thing is worth being, seeing that no object whatsoever should be grasped at and clung to as being a self or as belonging to self; as being good or bad, attractive or repulsive.

Insight meditation

This meditation is more conducive to insight than the four-stage approach but it's a little harder to maintain concentration. As with the four-stage meditation the focus of attention starts on the breath; we then label each in-breath 'rising' and each out-breath 'falling'. When sensations or thoughts arise, we don't resist them, but label them, saying slowly to ourselves, 'feeling, feeling, feeling' or, 'thinking, thinking, thinking'. We allow the thoughts and sensations to arise, have being and then pass away in their own time. And we return to labelling the breath.

As we perceive our attention wander from our breath we make a mental acknowledgement: if we feel an ache we note, 'hurting, hurting, hurting' until the ache subsides; if we start reliving an argument we label our memories, 'remembering, remembering, remembering' before returning to our breath. If we hear a distracting noise we note, 'hearing, hearing, hearing' and if we start wondering what we'll make for dinner we label, 'planning, planning, planning'.

Other mental experiences we may note might include: resenting, relaxing, resisting, smiling, wishing, longing—whatever arises. If we find ourselves struggling to find the perfect label it might be best to limit ourselves to the most basic categories, such as 'thinking' and 'feeling'. We use '-ing' words because they suggest a process and all mind states are processes which eventually turn into different processes.

If we feel a pain, an itch or any uncomfortable sensation we watch it, and our reaction to it, until it disappears. If it doesn't disappear quickly, we can scratch or adjust our position, but try to resist the temptation to respond unthinkingly to every physical sensation. In meditation, discomfort becomes something positive, for it's hard to ignore and forces us to be aware of the present moment. Discomfort is also an opportunity for us to practise *being* with our suffering and discomfort, to face it rather than fleeing it.

Meditators who grow frustrated with their minds' wandering appreciate insight meditation because everything that happens becomes part of the meditation, so distracting thoughts, sounds and sensations feel less frustrating. By developing our ability to label mental processes we increase our control over them. We become less likely to go on their journey, or identify too closely with them. We gradually learn to resist judging anything that arises as good or bad, and this is a useful skill for developing our patience with whatever life presents us.

Hindrances

Meditating can be enjoyable, relaxing, wondrous and blissful. Sometimes it can be the opposite. Establishing a meditation practice may not be smooth-sailing. A new meditator experiences frustration at the way their mind keeps wandering and doubts about the value of meditation. Or they could find themself 'not in the mood'. As they try to focus on their breath using the four-stage meditation, they might find their mind working like this:

'One, two, my foot's itchy . . . should I scratch it? I wonder if my foot's fully healed after that injury. Stop it! . . . three, four, five . . . oh no I didn't send that letter, now what am I going to do, oops . . . six, seven, I wonder if I'm doing this right . . . I certainly stuffed up the meditation yesterday . . . stop thinking! This isn't working . . .'

With practice, concentration improves, distractions are fewer and the beginner develops more confidence. Soon they start to notice how developing mindfulness enriches their life and this motivates them to persist through the more difficult days. With commitment, they eventually reach a point where meditation becomes as natural as showering or cleaning their teeth and they yearn for it if they miss a day.

Interestingly, in *Eight Mindful Steps to Happiness, Walking The Buddhas's Path*, the Thai author Gunaratana comments that Westerners starting meditation can be too severe with themselves; he describes them as, 'ambitious, driven, goal-oriented and insecure'. He continues:

'They clamp down on the mind and try to make it behave by sheer force of will . . . often they become self-judging and harsh.' He points out that we should meditate to 'watch' the mind, not 'control' it.

Knowing his followers would struggle with meditation, the Buddha warned of the five hindrances or obstacles that we can expect to meet. These are:

1. Distracting thoughts.
2. Ill-will, such as anger or other dark moods.
3. Sleepiness.
4. Restlessness.
5. Doubt.

A qualified teacher can advise us on how to deal with the obstacles that trouble us.

I remember when I first started meditating, my mind seemed to be so prone to wandering off into daydreams, so incapable of stillness that a sitting could feel like a waste of time. It took a couple of months of solid practice to feel some progress, to find more space between the thoughts, to learn that I could reach a place of stillness that could replenish me.

Cultivating the Mind of Love

To possess a mind of love is to recognise that all living beings are precious. It's helpful to remember that preciousness does not dwell in objects but in our minds. Consider the two objects, a diamond and a bowl of water. Which one is more precious? To the mind of someone lost in the desert the bowl of water is more precious. To the mind of a jeweller, a diamond is more precious. Preciousness is subjective, a quality of mind rather than a quality of the object. To love people we need a loving mind more than we need people to act lovably. Our love for others won't depend on their personal characteristics, behaviour or relationship with us but on our loving minds.

We can even love 'difficult' people, if for no other reason than for their role in our lives as spiritual teachers. For this we can be grateful. If our lives were full of likeable people, we'd be short of opportunities to grow wiser. But it's not only difficult people we can love for this reason—we can feel gratitude towards everyone we meet because they are all capable of making us wiser, they all provide us with opportunities to train ourselves in the mind of love.

Loving kindness meditation is a way to cultivate the mind of love by wishing ourselves and others well. Sending loving kindness is a way to transform your mind into one capable of loving all living beings. In doing this, others may eventually benefit in highly practical ways because there's someone in their lives who cares about them and wants the best for them.

We start by developing feelings of loving kindness for ourselves. We then do the same for a loved one followed by someone we don't know very well and then someone we don't particularly like. We conclude by sending loving kindness to all living beings, starting with those in close proximity and gradually widening to include the whole world. As you focus on each person you remind yourself that, just like you, they want to be happy and free from suffering and unhappiness, that we're all connected through this shared urge.

Whereas with mindfulness meditation we observe any thoughts but return our attention to the breath, in loving kindness meditation we need to think actively and creatively. For example, with the difficult person, we may need to think about the suffering and dissatisfaction in their life before we can feel compassion. It may take some reflection on their situation—their struggles, their disappointments—before we can acknowledge that this person is precious.

Loving kindness meditation

To start, you close your eyes, relax and prepare to focus. To slow down your thinking and still your mind you might start by being mindful of the breath.

1. In the first stage you work on cultivating loving kindness towards yourself. It's easier to love others when you have kind feelings for yourself. You might start with a contemplation of the goodness within, focussing on, say, a recent act of kindness. Buddhists use an infinite variety of thoughts and images to develop loving kindness, often using images of the Buddha or rays of light. The most common technique is to use phrases such as:

   May I be well.
   May I be free from suffering.
   May I be free from greed, hatred and delusion.
   May I live lovingly.
   May I be safe.
   May I be happy.
   May I become wise and compassionate.

2. After some time focussing on self-love you move to the second stage, where you send loving kindness to **someone you love.** Visualising a child, a family member or a close friend, wish for their happiness.

   May they experience love.
   May they feel joy.

3. You then turn your attention, in the third stage, to a **neutral person** for whom you have neither positive nor negative feelings. This could be a local shopkeeper, a member of the public, someone at work. You may never have spoken to this person but you send them loving kindness, perhaps drawing on some of the good feeling you enjoyed in the previous stage for the person you love. Sending loving kindness to a neutral person is a way to practise loving people regardless of what they can do for you personally.

4. In the fourth stage, you select **someone you find difficult** to get along with, often referred to as an 'enemy'. You can choose anyone towards whom your feelings are less than friendly. How can you find compassion for them? You could consider their positive qualities. Picture them as a precious child loved by their mother. Imagine their suffering, their anxieties and disappointments. Recognise that the behaviour that disturbs you may arise out of suffering or pain. Take inspiration from your reaction as a mother when your child acts in ways that are angry or selfish—your love for them doesn't diminish. Generally, however, teachers advise us to save the really difficult people, who may have wounded you deeply, until you are more experienced with the meditation. At this point in the meditation it can become challenging to keep your mind from wandering away, but as always, when you notice distracting thoughts you patiently bring your attention back to the task.

5. Finally, you work on sending loving kindness to **all beings** in the world, starting with those in close proximity or whom you already know and gradually widening to include everyone in your country, the world and then all living beings. Nurture a heartfelt wish that all living beings be happy and free from suffering and unhappiness.

Removing our focus from selfish concerns, we begin to think of others with kindness as we overcome feelings of separation. Of course, it might take many years to transform our mind into one that is truly loving, especially as we begin to work on our more difficult relationships. But even a beginner can start to feel like a more loving person within a short period of practising loving kindness meditation. Ideas of ways to help people may bubble into our consciousness during the meditation. Perhaps we might remember to phone or send a card to someone who is celebrating or suffering. Many meditators like to finish the meditation by thinking of one act of kindness they will carry out in the subsequent few hours.

Bowing

Some meditators find it useful while practising loving kindness meditation to picture themselves bowing before the person to whom they're sending loving kindness. For many Westerners the idea of bowing jars at first, but our reaction depends on the associations we make with bowing—it's not as if we're lowly urchins bowing for a tyrannical king, a fearsome God or some magical power.

For many Buddhists, bowing is simply an expression of respect and gratitude. To bow is to honour a person's dignity, humanity and preciousness. It feels humbling, but in the most positive way, as we suspend any tendency to be judgemental and superior, and feelings of compassion arise not from pity but from heartfelt esteem for a precious living being. We can also see bowing as an expression of gratitude for all that this person, be they beloved or belligerent, teaches us. We bow in gratitude for their potential to make us wiser and for the opportunity they give us to practise love.

An image I find useful is to imagine the Buddha placing his hands just above my head and channelling great torrents of loving kindness. I then imagine myself placing my hands just above the heads of others as I send them loving kindness.

When to practise loving kindness meditation

One of the purposes of loving kindness meditation is to cultivate our capacity to love all beings: ourselves, our loved ones, neutral people and difficult people. Since this is so difficult, we practise loving kindness meditation as often as we possibly can. Again, for a mother, where do we find the time? Yet loving kindness meditation is a practice which transfers easily to daily life. Ideally, we find time to practise it as a sitting meditation but it's just as valuable to send out love as we interact with others or even as we walk around the shops and streets. We can direct loving kindness to anyone we see. It feels strange at first but doesn't take long to feel normal and it certainly beats walking along consumed in our own thoughts. Achieving wonders for our state of mind, we find we have more positive feelings and energy to meet the demands of our day.

I find loving kindness meditation particularly useful before and during any social gathering. It helps me to:

- listen attentively and refrain from interrupting;
- speak more kindly;
- be aware of ways I can help others;
- avoid rambling on self-indulgently offering no benefit to the listener;
- enjoy myself as I feel less self-conscious, less self-absorbed.

Sending loving kindness is also useful before and during a day in the workplace or any event where we need to interact with others. It heightens our sensitivity to what others are experiencing, so that we might become a valuable person wherever we go.

Finding time for meditation

Finding the time to meditate will perhaps present a greater challenge to mothers than any challenge they meet during meditation. But given the benefits of meditation, is there something you could drop from your schedule? The time could come from skipping some TV shows—the average person views two to three hours of TV each day. Although mothers probably bring this average down, even if you only watch half an hour a day, you'd benefit enormously from meditating instead. Or the time to meditate might come from dropping your standards of housework, waking earlier or sending your family on a regular outing without you.

As a mother of young children Chittaprabha, from the Western Buddhist Order, was a committed meditator, rising early in the morning and, when her children were older, attending weekend or week-long retreats. She insists that she was able to be a far better mother by taking this time.

> Meditation is a way not only to attend to my own needs but to develop an awareness of others so that I can participate in all that I do in a more positive and creative way. Becoming more aware of the broader meaning of my life and of my true nature leads to a deeper sense of joy, contentment and equanimity from which everyone around me benefits.
>
> The aim is to take the awareness that we develop through meditation and allow it to permeate our whole life. As a mother such awareness helped me to see how I interacted with my children and the effects of my actions. So instead of repeating mistakes in an old habitual manner I could use awareness to bring about positive change and let go of a fixed and unchanging way of parenting.
>
> Being a parent can be a very important and enriching aspect of our lives, but our lives go beyond this. If I devoted all my attention to my children's desires, I would only be focussed on my immediate world and I'd be giving up the opportunity to become a true individual. When I embraced the wider perspective available through meditation I became more creative, free and responsive to the whole of life around me and less grasping and attached to my children and the things that brought me pleasure.
>
> The pleasure of loving and interacting spontaneously with children lessened if I tried to hold on too tightly. So I've always tried to seek a range of wholesome sources of pleasure, at the same time avoiding any grasping attachment to those pleasures.

Her two daughters, Michelle and Cara, laugh as they remember telling their mother at times throughout their childhood, 'Mum, I think it's time for you to go on another retreat.' Amusingly, many Buddhist parents report that it's often their children who remind them to take some time to meditate.

Chittaprabha also makes the point that to raise responsible, considerate children we need to teach them awareness and respect for the needs of others, including those of their parents. Although this is trickier when our children are young and egocentric, eventually they need to understand our need for some space to ourselves.

Chittaprabha urges all mothers to find some time every day, even if it's one minute, to reflect on something higher than themselves and their immediate lives:

> We make some time in each day where we can aspire to be our greatest selves. It might be a time to read and reflect on a short verse. We might light some candles or incense to offer to the Buddha. Or we meditate. And if we are not making this time we could ask ourselves what will inspire us to do so? For some it might be nature. Or it could be reading? Talking to our spiritual friends? Involvement in a spiritual community?

It's worth remembering that in developing mindfulness, we might gain more time in our day. As we've discussed, with a more focussed and clear mind we use our time more effectively, and find more energy. Many meditators claim they can survive on less sleep, the deep levels of concentration they attain in meditation providing a higher quality of rest.

CHAPTER 10

putting *it into* practice

Holding the baby, I stopped stirring the pot to answer the phone. Straining to hear over the general commotion of dinner time I was able to catch her words:

'Oliver has been complaining that he doesn't want to see Zac anymore because Zac keeps hurting him and he doesn't want to go to Zac's party. That's why we haven't been seeing you so much lately—Oliver just doesn't want to go near Zac because he's afraid of getting hurt. I haven't actually seen Zac hurting him but it wouldn't be like Oliver to make it up and he has commented two or three times now. Oliver isn't physical like that at all and he doesn't like it. I thought it best to tell you.'

Oliver was Zac's favourite friend in the world. I thought back to Oliver's fourth birthday party the week before and remembered how Oliver seemed to be ignoring Zac, walking away whenever Zac came near him. In a state of shock and confusion I replied:

'Well thanks so much for letting me know. It can't have been easy for you to tell me. You're very brave and I'm glad you didn't just sit on the information. I don't know what to say—I've never seen Zac hurt him either.'

Feeling satisfied with what I felt had been a calm, measured response, I hung up the phone and proceeded to go to pieces, announcing to my husband, 'We've got a crisis on our hands!'

Was my son secretly violent and sadistic as our four-year-old informer was suggesting? I knew that if struck, Zac would strike back. I knew he was 'physical' and at times rough, but I'd rarely seen him attack anybody unprovoked. I found myself growing angry with Oliver: he'd obviously turned against Zac and wanted to make him suffer. Then I was angry with his mother: how could she accept the word of a four year old who was certainly no angel himself? Besides, all the boys at Oliver's party seemed to be rough, ramming into each other on the jumping castle. Then again, maybe she and her son were completely justified. I felt confused.

The next day, I rang Zac's preschool teacher who told me that Zac was as rough as any of the boys his age and that although she'd seen him lose his temper and strike out he was 'definitely one of the milder ones'. We had to concede that at home Zac had recently become more short-tempered but we'd put it down to the arrival of testosterone. I decided it was best to tell Zac the bad news—maybe he needed to learn something. Besides, he kept asking to see Oliver. Zac denied he'd ever hit Oliver, then claimed Oliver had hit him first, then he had a little cry. I was no closer to knowing the truth but was glad the sad news didn't seem to do any deep psychological damage to Zac.

For the best part of 24 hours I felt quite depressed about that phone call. Sitting in front of the nightly news I listened to stories of Afghani refugees arriving back home after two years in leaky boats and detention centres, and there I was anguished by a tiff between two four year olds. I had satisfied myself that Zac did not have more than a mild problem with aggression that, if monitored, would disappear. So why did I overreact like that? Why did I cling to a negative mind state that made me feel unhappy? It came down to the second Noble Truth of Buddhism. Desire—or in this case it's flipside, aversion—causes suffering.

Applying Buddhism to a mother's quandary

I stubbornly wanted the world to be other than it was. I wanted my son to behave like a pacifist. I wanted him to have a best friend, devoted and loyal. Watching Oliver and Zac play together had always warmed my heart. What was hurting me most though was my desire for Zac to never experience rejection. Examining my thoughts with mindfulness I could see that this episode had teased out my own pain from times past when friends had suddenly taken an unexplained dislike to me, leaving me frustrated and hurt. I never wanted Zac to experience this part of life, especially not at the tender age of four, and this incident was forcing me to face this fear. The irony was that while I was busy sulking, Zac was getting on with life, playing kangaroos with the children next door.

So how did practising Buddhism help me through this? Ten years ago, I'm sure I would have acted defensively on the phone, attacking the other mother with accusations about how her son was treating mine. But Buddhism has brought me to admit that every time I've ever responded angrily I've done harm, not least to myself. Buddhism helps me to resist the pull of automatic reactions such as denial, blaming and defensiveness, and take a deeper look at what's going on. The challenge was to see these events with clarity rather than defend my ground.

My practice allowed me to watch the inner journey of this mini-drama so that I could identify all the thoughts, beliefs and emotions fuelling my unhappiness. It was an opportunity for spiritual practice, showing me what I cling to and requiring me to let go and make room for patient acceptance of anything I couldn't fix.

Buddhism has also taught me not to jump to conclusions and cling to my views. Rather than denying Zac's potential for aggression, as I'd like to, I have to keep my mind open to all possibilities and monitor his behaviour through this phase. Rather than demonise Oliver's family, I say 'I don't know' and surrender to the ever-unfolding mystery of it all.

Then again, some would say I think too much. And they're dead right. What I really needed was time out on my meditation cushion and over the weekend that followed I managed to find 40 minutes for uninterrupted meditation. Starting with mindfulness of the breath meditation I managed to bask in some stillness, some spaciousness. Inspired by some recent teachings I then worked on my determination to be happier, slowly repeating, 'I will transform my mind', as a way to stop surrendering to negative mind states. After this sitting not only did I feel calm and revitalised, but the whole episode suddenly became a vague memory and I wondered why I had ever made such a fuss. As my wise mother-in-law said with a shrug, *'Czasami dzieci się kłuca. Zdarza się'*, which is Polish for 'Kids fight. It happens'. Although my wound can at times reopen when my son asks to see his friend, I feel that my practice helps me to deal with the issue like a grown-up.

So what is Buddhism again?

Perhaps in response to the vastness and complexity of modern Buddhism, with its 2500 years of history in a variety of cultures, there have been several attempts to summarise it, to reduce it to one catchy message. Some describe Buddhism simply as mindfulness or awakening to the present moment. In the words of fifteenth-century Zen master Ikkyu:

> Attention. Attention. Attention.

Another summary of Buddhism offered earlier in this book refers to our potential to substitute our usual thoughts and actions with more wholesome alternatives:

> Stopping and realising.

Some describe Buddhism as:

> The cultivation of wisdom and compassion.

This summary is usually accompanied by the observation that there can be no wisdom without compassion and no compassion without wisdom.

In Buddhism our access to that which is divine is through the heart: Buddhism is about love. The Dalai Lama often says:

> My religion is kindness.

Others would describe Buddhism as the four Noble Truths together with the Noble Eightfold Path, or as the Buddha concisely put it:

> I teach suffering and the end of suffering.

The Eightfold Path requires us not to limit our practice to a meditation session, nicely compartmentalised from the rest of our lives, but to extend our awareness to every aspect of our lives so that we live every moment as mindfully, compassionately and ethically as possible. A more concise way of summarising this idea comes in my own favourite summary of Buddhism:

> Learn to do good. Cease to do harm. Purify the mind.

Many Buddhists commit this one to memory and use it as a mantra throughout the day or for a meditation session. It's a soothing summary to come back to when you feel yourself becoming overstimulated by the impressive array of teachings.

What I particularly like about Buddhism

With its long history and wide range of cultural settings, it's unsafe to generalise about the way people practise Buddhism for there will be an exception to anything you say. Still, I'd like to make some generalisations based on my own experience, although I'm sure there are those who would debate them.

Buddhism treats you like an adult. It's not a religion. You don't need to believe anything unless it fits with your own personal experience. You use your judgement, inspired by wisdom and compassion, rather than follow a set of sacred thou-shalts. Spiritual progress is your responsibility. You set the pace. In Buddhism there is no God, no Creator, no judge to set rules, watch you and assess your behaviour. For many it comes as a relief to hear that Buddhists work not so much against 'sin' as delusion. And you deal with delusion not through guilt and suppression but awareness and insight. The Buddha did not seek blind faith from his followers but the opposite: a questioning approach. In the Buddha's words:

Do not accept anything because:

1. Of repeated oral transmission.
2. Of lineage or tradition.
3. It has been widely stated.
4. It has been written in books, such as scriptures.
5. It is logical and reasonable.
6. Of inferring and drawing conclusions.
7. It has been thought out.
8. Of acceptance and conviction through a theory.
9. The speaker appears competent.
10. Of respect for the teacher.

Know what things would be censured by the wise and which, if pursued, would lead to harm and suffering.

Encouraged to question, his followers develop their own wisdom. The emphasis is on inquiry, trying teachings out for yourself and putting them through the test of your own personal experience.

The Buddha didn't expect us to blindly embrace all Buddhist teachings. Personally, I can't quite accept the concept of reincarnation even though other Buddhists I know find it 'obvious', or 'perfectly logical'. It's not that I can present any compelling evidence against it, but when it comes to death my overriding feeling is that I just don't know. I'm grateful my reservations about this belief will never see me excluded from Buddhist circles.

The Buddha hardly sounds like the leader of a 'religion', for example, in this quotation:

I am not teaching you to have you as my pupil. I am not interested to make you my pupil. I am not interested in breaking you from your old teacher. I am not interested even to change your goal, because everyone wants to come out of sufferings. Try something that I have discovered, and then judge it for yourself. If it is good for you, accept it. Otherwise, don't accept it.

Humans being humans, there are Buddhists who have squeezed their Buddhism into a more religious shape. As with all systems, some have found ways to make Buddhism political, sexist or obscured by rituals. Buddhism has been practised in so many countries for so many years that it has collected some exotic bells and whistles. But these are always secondary to the main teachings and you can ignore them if they don't support your practice.

Buddhists don't need to produce converts. There's no need to 'save' people, offer your firstborn or argue your partner into submission. My own husband, a committed atheist, has not the slightest interest in Buddhism and probably never will. Yet our different standpoints have never been a source of conflict, rather of lively, stimulating discussion. In making me calmer and happier, Buddhism has in fact done more to nurture our partnership than polarise us.

A religion can provide comforting 'answers' to all those meaning-of-life questions. In Buddhism, you find guidelines on how to discover your own answers and perhaps more importantly your questions—for life is seen as a series of mysteries. Buddhism encourages us to be open to every new experience without automatically applying all our prejudices and tired opinions. As the eminent Zen Master Shunryu Suzuki said, 'In the beginner's mind there are many possibilities, but in the expert's there are few.'

The need to slow down

When we are too plain busy we have no time to absorb the present moment, notice our surroundings or meditate. Nor do we have space to reflect on our lives, analyse where we're going and whether we even want to go there. Busyness undermines our capacity for acts of love by robbing us of time to listen to others, notice how they're feeling and help them. To quote the Buddha:

The restless, busy nature of the world, this, I declare, is at the root of pain. Attain that composure of mind which is resting in the peace of immortality. Self is but a heap of composite qualities, and its world is empty like a fantasy.

Those of us who juggle career and kids know that when we're stressed over our workload, spending time with our children can be exasperating. It's so trying to spend time at a park when there's 'important work' to do. When you become too obsessed with productivity it's hard to adapt to the children's pace, to be present and accepting of the present moment.

Sometimes we have little choice but to be busy—family life seems to require this of us. But at other stages in our lives, we need to ask, could we be burying ourselves in activity to avoid facing the big questions? Do we find it so difficult to cope with unstructured time that we set our lives up to avoid it? If this is the case, what is the price of our addiction to busyness? For many the price is a feeling of disconnection from those around them and from any chance of fostering the kind of families and communities that humans so profoundly need. Or the price could be disconnection from ourselves, addiction to stress or a failure to find joy in life.

We need to create some space in our lives if we want to progress along a spiritual path. Before children, when life became too troubling we might have thrown ourselves into our work, started new hobbies or lost ourselves in a social whirl—anything to distract ourselves from facing time alone with our thoughts. Now we are parents and in danger of neglecting our children if we chase these time-consuming distractions. We need to find ways to live in harmony with ourselves and our families.

Creating time

What would it take to create some time for spiritual pursuits such as meditation, spiritual study, enjoying nature or being fully present to listen to someone? Reducing the hours we spend in front of TV? Resisting the impulse to turn on the radio? Spending less time in idle chatter? It's not uncommon as people advance along a spiritual path to make major lifestyle changes to create more time. People throw in their unsatisfying jobs, move away from their expensive neighbourhood, sell cumbersome assets, end destructive relationships, scale down their social lives or spend less money.

To what extent could we all simplify our lives? Tidy up? Give stuff away? Reduce the time we spend consuming the 'News' (so much of which we forget)? Does the way we entertain ourselves keep our life pacey or does it help you to slow down and develop inner peace? Several times the Buddha advised us to be 'moderate in eating'. We can eat plainer food instead of food that saps our energy, get enough sleep and exercise. The Buddha urged us to look after our health as a way to ensure we have the energy for spiritual development:

> *To keep the body in good health is a duty, for otherwise we shall not be able to trim the lamp of wisdom, and keep our mind strong and clear.*

It helps if we regularly ask ourselves: how would I spend this day, week or month if I knew it was my last? In other words, what really matters and what is mere bustle? If we can learn what we need to be happy, we can stop wasting energy on our delusions. It also helps to recognise that what we really want from life is not so much the external objects or experiences, but the positive mind states that we associate with them. Wouldn't it be wiser to seek that mind state from inner work instead of chasing the externals? It reminds me of that joke: 'If half the fun of a holiday is planning it, then just stay home and plan two!'

If we managed to rearrange our lives a little, remove some of the clutter, what might this new space bring us?

We could enjoy time for silence, stillness, meditation. We might watch our children sleeping, gaze into the eyes of our baby, go for a walk, observe nature, write in a diary, enjoy a slow meal, or listen to all the sounds around us. We might do something utterly spontaneous: pick some flowers, chat to a stranger, go for a leisurely wander to explore a neighbourhood. These activities allow us to reconnect with ourselves and find energy. They also remind us that life can be lighter, more spontaneous and enjoyable.

Finding a spiritual community

From time to time we might catch a glimpse of a better way to live, of the greater person we could become, or perhaps of what we are doing wrong. Moments of lucidity. They might come from reading a book, finding some time for reflection or meeting someone who inspires us. The important question is: how can we make these moments of inspiration actually amount to something? How can we change our lives in a lasting way? If we read the occasional book about Buddhism we are left with a practice that comes and goes and does little for us at any deep level. We end up using Buddhism as one more way to make us feel good, something to revisit every six months, or every few years.

For those interested in committing to spiritual progress, the answer is to join a spiritual community. When we receive regular teachings from a qualified teacher and meet with others who are trying to apply these teachings, motivation can cease to be an issue. The Three Treasures the Buddha said could sustain us on our spiritual path are the *Buddha* (who inspires us to awaken), the *Dharma* (his teachings) and the *Sangha* (the spiritual community).

An author who has studied with Tibetan lamas for over 20 years, Julie Henderson, gives this interesting explanation for why we need a *sangha*:

> We are extraordinarily influenced by primate and tribal needs. What this means practically is that we want very much to fit in with those around us. We are far more likely to take on the

> states of being of the folks around us than we are to create 'cleaner' states on our own. Even when the states of the people around us are miserable and unpleasant, it is simply easier to participate in them as they are than to make our own, separate from theirs. Noticing this has led to an understanding of sangha as that group of people who actively and consciously pursue embodiment of the four primary states and, in so doing, make it easier for all to do so.

It takes strength to resist the messages our materialistic society bombards us with and the people around us might not question such messages. Often enough we live with people who think they can find happiness from cars, money, property, beauty and youth, and it's easy to absorb such values ourselves. How refreshing it is to immerse ourselves in a culture where the values are deeper than this, values such as loving kindness, compassion, sympathetic joy and equanimity.

Choosing a tradition

On my weekly 'night off' from family duties, I used to enjoy touring around my city looking at the different Buddhist schools on offer. One night I'd be chanting in Tibetan, another night walking slowly around a candlelit room with 50 people in walking meditation. At one centre I'd be on a journey with creative visualisations and at the next one I'd be sending out loving kindness to all living beings. Meeting the different teachers and practitioners was as stimulating as it was fascinating.

To start on our spiritual path seriously, however, we need to commit to one teacher from one school of Buddhism, otherwise we skim about the surface of several practices rather than going deeply into one. In Buddhism, 'lineage' is the key word when it comes to choosing a teacher. A qualified teacher comes from a long line of teacher–student relationships stretching back to the Buddha himself. Within each lineage there are likely to be courses of study, or other programs which we can follow to a level to suit ourself. We can take it as seriously as we need to, choosing a path to full ordination or just dropping in occasionally to hear some teachings.

Our choices of a school are likely to be: Zen, Tibetan or Theravadan. In essence the core message is the same in all Buddhist schools, the difference usually lying more in the approach to practice. It might even be wiser to choose a *sangha* based on our rapport with the teacher rather than on the school of Buddhism. Realistically, for mothers the choice may come down to convenience as we settle on the closest school or the easiest time slot.

We can make some generalisations about the differences between the schools but since Buddhism tends to adapt to the culture it settles in, generalisations can only be rough. A Western orientation to any of these schools is likely to downplay rules, rituals and customs. Without exploring the schools *within* each of these schools, we can tentatively make the following generalisations.

Tibetan Buddhism probably provides the most exotic extras in the way of chanting and statues and rituals, possibly due to the Tibetans' attempts to salvage their threatened culture. Most of the recently established Western Buddhist centres in Australia are Tibetan. With its emphasis on kindness, the Tibetan school is the most altruistic of the traditions, all efforts to attain enlightenment being with a view to helping all living beings. Interestingly, Tibetan Buddhism differs from the other schools in its appreciation for the scriptures, for learning, memorising, debating and using the intellect. It also makes greater use of creative visualisation or imagery in meditation.

Theravadan Buddhism is practised in Sri Lanka, Thailand, Laos, Cambodia and Burma, and is often seen as the simplest of the traditions with the least ritual. It emphasises the importance of achieving insight during meditation by mindfully observing distractions rather than forcing them out of our consciousness. The Theravadan school is seen as a purer form of Buddhism because it uses the oldest and most original of the Buddhist scriptures.

Zen Buddhism, practised mainly in China, Korea and Japan, could be described as the most rigorous school, emphasising hard work and struggle in meditation. The popular Vietnamese monk Thich Nhat Hanh, on the other hand, heads a school of Zen Buddhism which some find gentle and relatively easy for a Westerner to slip into. Traditional Zen is also quite anti-intellectual, seeing books, discussions, thinking and teaching as distractions to true practice. Although compassion is an important part of Zen, the main emphasis is on developing one's ability to be present for the here and now. Rinzai Zen Buddhism is well-known for using *koans* which meditators must spend hours, weeks or months solving. The most famous example must be, 'What is the sound of one hand clapping?' The purpose of koans is to prove the limitations of the rational mind and the need to transcend it in order to gain insight.

The path of a practising parent

The fourteenth-century Indian sage Shantideva poses the question, Given all the thistles, thorns and rocks, why cover the whole world with leather when you could use a pair of sandals? In the same way, why try to change the world when we could just change the mind? But it takes us a long time to learn the futility of forcing life to be other than it is. We don't easily give up our unrealistic hopes of arranging our lives to avoid suffering and the unsatisfactory. We have years of conditioning to overcome and some well-entrenched delusions to root out. We may need to practise mindfulness for years before we even become aware of some of our delusions. We need to remind ourselves regularly that the world outside us fails to deliver lasting, reliable happiness, that we need to strive for inner peace. Buddhism teaches us that romance, wealth, achievement and relationships all cause us misery if we grasp at them with desirous attachment. To be happy we need to transform our minds.

Parents have a head start when it comes to giving up on the external world to deliver happiness: our children won't let us participate in it to anywhere near the extent we'd like to. They force us to stop chasing external happiness and to instead spend rainy days in our living rooms, sunny days at playgrounds, cloudy days pacing shopping malls. By removing so many of the distractions from our lives they require us to turn inward for happiness. And so often they hold up a mirror for us to see what our minds are really like. Sometimes it's not a pretty sight and we realise what we need to work on. Yes, children are the most demanding and merciless of spiritual teachers.

Again and again our children turn us into amateurs. As they move from phase to phase our ability to cope with what's going on will vary from month to month, along with our ability and commitment to practise Buddhist teachings. But if we can develop some inner peace, some equanimity, what is happening outside us has less potential to overexcite or upset us. With inner peace we create some space between external events and our response to them. And this can only make us more helpful to our children as we parent them attentively and provide better role models.

On starting to put Buddhist teachings into practice you might find many aspects of your life improve dramatically. Some changes are easy to implement—it doesn't stretch us too far to be a little friendlier to people in our community, more loving to our family members and more positive in our outlook. Within a very short time we might be impressed by how Buddhist practice has improved our life. But we must be ready for the plateau—many aspects of our life only show progress after years of practice. We might need many years to rid our minds of harmful thoughts, forgive those who have wounded us and conquer negative mind states.

Nobody finds the journey along a spiritual path a straight line of progress; life still has its highs and lows and with them our commitment travels through peaks and troughs. Our emotional life may even become worse before it gets better. Uncovering hidden or suppressed wounds is uncomfortable and can trigger unexpected emotional reactions. Healing is highly likely to be our first priority after years of denying or ignoring inner pain. In the long run we can only benefit from the internal spring cleaning of any mess that blocks our joy in living.

In the widely-read book *After the Ecstasy, the Laundry*, Jack Kornfield, who has practised and taught Buddhism for decades, writes:

> For almost everyone who practises . . . times of profound peace and newfound love are often overtaken by periods of loss, by closing up, fear, or the discovery of betrayal, only to be followed again by equanimity or joy.

A spiritual path does not provide an escape from the suffering in life and may even rub our noses in it. Yet over time we are sure to note progress in all areas of our lives as our minds become healthier places.

In closing . . .

Since meditation is so powerful, why not throw our energies into this and forget the Buddhist part? People everywhere are making a commitment to meditation for the sake of their health, stress management or to help them achieve their goals. But this raises the question, 'What kind of world do I want to live in?' One where everyone pursues self-improvement and tries to make the world more comfortable for Number One? Or would I prefer a world of interconnected beings who care about each other, serve their communities, love and help others?

One way to address the isolation and lack of community in modern life is to favour an orientation which considers more than ourselves and our own limited world. Rather than foster a culture of meditators who can only achieve higher states of consciousness, heal themselves and achieve their worldly goals, I want to be part of a movement that enables us to reconnect with each other as well, one that recognises the preciousness and vulnerability of human beings. In Buddhism, compassion for others is the way to connect to the divine.

Words will never capture the enormity of the Truth that we all overlook—they can provide a hint but will always be inadequate to describe the potential of what we can experience and who we can be. Buddhism teaches that with love we can be so much more than a body made up of its five senses and its rational mind, that we have a great deal more potential than we realise. Always acknowledging the suffering and imperfection of our lives, Buddhist practice gives us pause for hope. Doubtless, it is this that makes Buddhism such a fast-growing and popular practice.

appendix 1: the noble eightfold path

THE NOBLE EIGHTFOLD PATH captures almost all Buddhist teachings. It's a way of life requiring discipline and it leads to liberation.

Wisdom

Skilful understanding

Skilful understanding means seeing life the way it is: understanding the four Noble Truths about suffering and the end of suffering, along with the truths of impermanence, and *no-self.* At first we may have an intellectual understanding of these truths but need only to look at how we live our lives to realise we lack a deep understanding. As we shed the impurities of our minds through meditation and spiritual growth we increase the potential for deep realisation of these truths.

Skilful thought

This is the intention to increase our awareness and purify our thoughts from greed, hatred and delusion. If we can gain some control over our thoughts, this takes care of many of our feelings and actions. We create our reality through our thinking—the quality of our experience of life depends enormously on the way we think. We have the choice to think our way into happiness or gloom, and the way we think can improve life for those around us or drag them down.

Ethics

Skilful speech

The Buddha said that skilful speech was *truthful, kind, gentle and helpful.* We should aim to say the right thing at the right time to the right person, so we need to be careful with what we say. When our speech might not be helpful or useful to the listener we need to exercise restraint. Refraining from the use of harsh language, we should avoid speech that is malicious, harmful or self-serving. We avoid gossiping and breaking confidences. We also consider whether what we say benefits the listener or wastes their time. (See page 136 for more on skilful speech.)

Skilful action

Our conduct needs to be ethical and compassionate, as do the intentions behind our conduct. With self-awareness we can discover what motivates our actions. Skilful action also includes abiding by the Five Precepts, namely:

1. Not to destroy life;
2. Not to steal;
3. Not to indulge in sexual misconduct;
4. Not to tell lies;
5. Not to take drugs or alcohol that can cloud our judgement.

How literally these precepts are applied varies from school to school and even within schools. As a general rule, it's more important to respond wisely and compassionately to each individual situation you confront than to follow rules.

Skilful livelihood

Buddhists need to make their living from work that does not cause harm to others. Specifically, we need to avoid professions that involve trading in weapons, selling intoxicating drinks, killing animals or cheating. Whether we are factory workers or accountants, we need to face areas of our livelihood which may conflict with our values. This might mean addressing issues affecting the health of our customers, the environment, the honesty of our advertising claims or the way we treat those we deal with.

Mental discipline

Skilful effort

Skilful effort is required both in meditation sittings and in our daily life. In meditation we don't furrow our brows and force ourselves to concentrate, with the discipline of the harshest school principal. Neither do we relax so much that we 'don't care' about our concentration, or that we fall asleep. We find instead a middle way between these extremes. In our daily life, skilful effort is about our will to encourage wholesome mind states and purify our minds from greed, hatred and delusion.

Skilful mindfulness

Mindfulness is about paying close attention, not only during a meditation sitting but also at every moment of our day. We need to learn to live meditatively, to focus on the constantly changing Now rather than on past conversations and events and rather than on our desires and fears for the future. The Buddha specified four levels of experience we need to be mindful of:

1. the body—its sensations, aches, itches, pains, tensions, pleasures;
2. our feelings—our emotions or mind states including anger, joy, sadness and peacefulness;
3. our thoughts—our plans, dreams, regrets, memories, judgements;
4. our attitudes to the universal laws of life—impermanence, no-self and non-separation.

Skilful concentration

Often referred to as one-pointedness, skilful concentration refers to the ability to focus on one aspect of experience without our minds becoming distracted. It's the achievement of control over our thinking.

appendix 2: helpful books

Why Buddhism? Westerners in Search of Wisdom
by Vicki Mackenzie
Around Sydney, I've found it hard to meet anyone interested in Buddhism who hasn't read this book. Based on 16 interviews with mainly high-profile Buddhists, Mackenzie probes each follower for what drew them to Buddhism and how it enriches their life. All Westerners, but from diverse backgrounds, their potted life stories are included, as well as their experience of Buddhism in their own words.

The Naked Buddha, A Simple Explanation of a 'New' Old Religion
by Adrienne Howley
Mother of two sons, in her early 70s, Adrienne Howley was ordained by the Dalai Lama in 1982. Her book is a 'primer' on Buddhism, emphasising the need to base your practice and all your beliefs on personal experience. After describing the key teachings of Buddhism she explores such topics as the monastic life and Buddhism in different cultures. She has an impressive knowledge of Buddhism as practised in both the East and the West and plenty of first-hand experience of both.

The Path to Peace Within, A Guide to Insight Meditation
by Helen Jandamit
A thin book, it provides an excellent summary of the steps involved in Theravadan insight meditation. It includes a thorough explanation of walking meditation. Jandamit also takes a few chapters to explain some of the core Buddhist teachings, and with her wealth of experience from teaching meditation in Thailand, she does this very clearly.

***Stumbling Toward Enlightenment* by Geri Larkin**
Sex in the City meets Buddhism. To make the point that practising Buddhism is superior to researching it, Geri Larkin speculates: 'Why read about great sex when you can just have it?' She also includes a chapter called 'When all you still think about is sex'. Mother of two, Geri Larkin was a highly paid management consultant working an average of 72 hours a week. She gradually reduced her working hours, sold her magnificent home and belongings and moved into a temple. This book makes enjoyable, light reading: it's packed with humour and Larkin is fascinatingly honest about her flaws, struggles and failures on the spiritual path. Very inspiring, motivating and reassuring.

Light on Enlightenment, Revolutionary Teachings on the Inner Life
by Christopher Titmuss
Christopher Titmuss was a journalist before he spent six years as a Buddhist monk in Thailand and India. More recently he has been a teacher, leading insight meditation retreats around the world. Although he is not a parent, I recommend his book for its clear presentation of Buddhist concepts. Each chapter bears a title such as, 'The Four Noble Truths', 'The Eight Worldly Conditions' or 'The Four Foundations of Awareness'. He illustrates the teachings with modern examples in easy-to-read language. After each teaching he includes a list of useful questions so the reader can do their own soul-searching, such as: 'Do you have vision, passion, interest and skill?', 'What is the motive for your primary activities?', 'Do you do things because you don't know what else to do?'

Lovingkindness, The Revolutionary Art of Happiness **and** ***A Heart as Wide as the World, Stories on the Path of Lovingkindness***
by Sharon Salzberg
Sharon Salzberg is one of the most popular Buddhist writers of our time. A founder of the famous Insight Meditation Society in Massachusetts, she has practised and taught meditation all over the world. Her great passion is for the Buddhist teachings about love, in particular the four Divine Abodes of loving kindness, compassion, sympathetic joy and equanimity. She writes so accessibly and so inspiringly that it's impossible to read her books without revolutionising your approach to all your relationships. She could create a kinder person out of the weariest of cynics. Drawing on her experiences in Russia, Burma, India, Thailand, Australia and her home in the United States, her personal stories are as moving as they are exotic.

Forgiveness and other Acts of Love **and** ***The Universal Heart***
by Stephanie Dowrick
Stephanie Dowrick is one of my favourite inspirational authors and these are my two favourites of her books. She writes about the subject of love in a way that is nothing short of rivetting. She makes living lovingly seem attractive and exciting. Drawing on a wealth of experience in psychotherapy, she weaves countless anecdotes into her arguments to illustrate her points. Despite encompassing wisdom from several spiritual traditions, including Buddhism, her books seem to me to present the Buddhist message. *Forgiveness and Other Acts of Love* provides a chapter on each of the six virtues of courage, fidelity, restraint, generosity, tolerance and forgiveness. *The Universal Heart* discusses the benefits of loving all people rather than a select handful, loving those close to us in a purer way and loving ourselves. Both books can be read many times over and dipped into for moments of inspiration.

***A Path with Heart, A Guide Through the Perils and Promises of Spiritual Life* and *After the Ecstasy, the Laundry, How the Heart Grows Wise on the Spiritual Path* by Jack Kornfield**
Jack Kornfield must have one of the most impressive résumés in the Buddhist world. Trained as a monk in Thailand, Burma and India, he has taught Buddhism since 1974. A prolific writer and co-founder of the renowned Insight Meditation Society, he has been pivotal in bringing Buddhist teachings to the West. He has a PhD in Psychology and one daughter. The way he presents his favourite topics of self-awareness, mindfulness and compassion is very accessible to the Western mind and he has plenty of experiences to draw on, having spoken intimately over the years with thousands of students, teachers and Buddhist bigwigs. His approach is realistic, simple and down-to-earth. He is also surprisingly open about his own personal struggles, with his father, his wife and his own demons.

***Peace of Mind* by Dr Ian Gawler**
Although not a Buddhist work, this book gives an overview of the benefits of meditation and the choice of techniques and approaches available. Dr Gawler divides meditation into three types: health meditation, insight meditation and creative meditation. He also presents seven levels of higher consciousness that we can achieve in meditation. It's a highly motivating book, so is particularly helpful at a time when we're experiencing doubts or a lapse in commitment to practice. Dr Gawler is interested in results rather than any spiritual focus and emphasises meditating for health benefits and stress management. This is understandable given his own successful battle with 'terminal' cancer ten years ago and his experience helping thousands learn to meditate in order to overcome their illnesses, in particular, cancer.

appendix 3: helpful websites

www.buddhanet.net

Run by the 60-year-old Australian monk, Pannyavaro, this is the world's largest Buddhist Internet site. Truly vast, it provides such resources as directories for Buddhist centres all over the world, audio talks, e-books, meditation instructions and plenty of introductory information. There are resources for children, including a Kid's Page, crossword puzzles, study materials and instructions on how to incorporate loving kindness meditation into the bedtime ritual. You can also find information about high-profile, female Buddhists, as well as discussions of the female role in Buddhism through history.

www.geocities.com/southbeach/pointe/5640/index1.html

This one is a real treasure. It contains profiles of Buddhists from all over the world who are looking for pen pals to provide support and discussion. The diversity of people listed here is truly amazing, spanning all ages, races, genders and life situations. Many people are looking for their own Buddhist cyber-community, others are looking for people in similar situations to themselves with whom they can discuss Buddhist teachings. Speaking from my own experience, it's very exciting to communicate with Buddhist mothers in different parts of the world. If you don't have time for a pen pal, this site is worth a visit if only to read the personal profiles, which often describe how people discovered Buddhism and how it helps them.

www.tricycle.com

Tricycle is a quarterly Buddhist magazine published in New York and its website seems infinite—you could easily spend a week there! Along with extracts from past issues of the magazine, there's information about 'Buddhist Basics' for beginners. On the 'Bulletin Boards', which attract hundreds of visitors, you can read and contribute to discussions on a wide range of topics, including any Buddhist concept imaginable, current world events and favourite Buddhist books.

www.serve.com/cmtan/buddhism/

This site is called 'What do you think, my friend? (Writings On Buddhism)' and contains articles, questions and answers, and many contributions from visitors about how they apply Buddhism in their lives. For those who want to go straight to the original source of Buddhist wisdom, it contains the 423 verses of the Dhammapada, the words of the Buddha.

appendix 4: from the scriptures

Sermon at Rajagaha

'Surrender the grasping disposition of selfishness, and you will attain to that calm state of mind which conveys perfect peace, goodness and wisdom . . .

'Do not deceive, do not despise
Each other anywhere.
Do not be angry, nor should you
Secret resentment bear;
For as a mother risks her life
And watches o'er her child,
So boundless be your love to all,
So tender, kind and mild.

'Indeed cherish goodwill right and left,
All round, early and late,
And without hindrance, without stint,
From envy free and hate,

While standing, walking, sitting down,
Whate'er you have in mind,
The rule of life that's always best
Is to be loving-kind.

'Gifts are great . . . meditations and religious exercises pacify the heart, comprehension of the truth leads to Nirvana, but greater than all is loving kindness. As the light of the moon is sixteen times stronger than the light of all the stars, so loving kindness is sixteen times more efficacious in liberating the heart than all other religious accomplishments taken together.'

(Verses 18–22 from the *Sermon at Rajagaha*)

Avoiding the Ten Evils

The Buddha said: 'All acts of living creatures become bad by ten things, and by avoiding the ten things they become good. There are three evils of the body, four evils of the tongue, and three evils of the mind.

'The evils of the body are, murder, theft and adultery; of the tongue, lying, slander, abuse and idle talk; of the mind, covetousness, hatred and error.

'I urge you to avoid the ten evils:

I. Do not kill, but have regard for life.
II. Do not steal, but help everybody to be master of the fruits of their labors.
III. Abstain from impurity and lead a life of chastity.
IV. Do not lie, but be truthful. Speak the truth with discretion, fearlessly and in a loving heart.
V. Do not invent evil reports, nor repeat them. Do not find fault, but look for the good sides of your fellow beings, so that you may with sincerity defend them against their enemies.
VI. Do not swear, but speak decently and with dignity.

VII. Do not waste time with gossip, but speak to the purpose or keep silence.

VIII. Do not covet, nor envy, but rejoice at the fortunes of other people.

IX. Cleanse your heart of malice and cherish no hatred, not even against your enemies; but embrace all living beings with kindness.

X. Free your mind of ignorance and be anxious to learn the truth, especially in the one thing that is needful in case you fall a prey either to scepticism or to errors. Scepticism will make you indifferent and errors will lead you astray, so that you shall not find the noble path that leads to life eternal.'

(Verses 1–13, *Avoiding the Ten Evils*)

appendix 5: buddhism for mothers of newborns

Mothering as Meditation Practice by Anne Cushman
(excerpt from Fall 2001 issue of *Tricycle* magazine, New York)

For the first few weeks of my son Skye's life, he would only sleep if he could hear my heartbeat. From midnight to dawn he lay on my chest, his head tucked into the hollow of my throat, awakening every two hours to nurse. In the day, he'd nap in my arms as I rocked, a slideshow of emotions—joy, exasperation, amusement, angst, astonishment—flickering across his dreaming face, as if he were rehearsing every expression he would need for the rest of his life. If I dared to set him in his bassinet, he'd wake up with a roar of outrage, red-faced and flailing. He cried if I tried to put him in a baby sling, frontpack, stroller, or car seat. He cried whenever I changed his diaper. And every evening from seven to nine, he cried for no apparent reason at all.

When Skye was two weeks old, I ate black bean tacos for dinner and he screamed until sunrise, his body stiff and his fists clenched. While I sobbed along with him, my husband actually called the emergency room, where the nurse on duty told us, kindly, that it sounded like gas. The next morning, a nutritionist friend assured me that everything would be fine so long as I stopped eating dairy, wheat, yeast, soy, corn, legumes, garlic, onions, tomatoes, sugar, peppers, broccoli, and citrus fruit (and considered dropping fish, mushrooms, and eggs). As Skye finally fell asleep in the crook of my right arm, I collapsed on the sofa in my bathrobe, eating cold brown rice with my left hand and spilling it in his hair.

It was about that time that I decided that what I had embarked on was an intensive meditation retreat. It had all the elements, I told myself: the long hours of silent sitting; the walking back and forth, going nowhere; the grueling schedule and sleep deprivation; the hypnotic, enigmatic chants ('. . . and if that looking glass gets broke/Mama's gonna buy you a billy goat . . .'); the slowly dawning realization that there is nothing to look forward to but more of the same. And at the center of it, of course, was the crazy wisdom teacher in diapers, who assigned more demanding practices than I had encountered in all my travels in India—like 'Tonight you will circumambulate the living room for two hours with the master in your arms, doing a deep-knee bend at every other step, and chanting, 'Dooty-dooty-doot-doot-doo, dooty-dooty-doot-doot-doo.' Or 'At midnight you will carry the sleeping master with you to the bathroom and answer this koan: How do you lower your pajama bottoms without using your hands?'

Like all great spiritual practices, these were exquisitely designed to rattle the cage of my ego. They smashed through my concepts about how things should be (rocking in the garden swing by the lavender bush, watching the hummingbirds, while my newborn slept in a bassinet by my feet) and pried open my heart to the way things actually were (standing by the diaper table, flexing one tiny knee after another into Skye's colicky tummy, and cheering when a mustard-yellow fountain erupted from his behind). And with every breath of my 'baby sesshin', I was offered the opportunity to cradle my child in my arms like the baby Buddha and be present for a mystery unfolding . . .

As a new mother, I've found myself wondering: How are other women negotiating the dance between practice and parenting? How does their practice affect their mothering? How does being a mother affect their practice? Are mothers changing the forms of Buddhism in America?

And—the most compelling question of all for me—can mothering really be a path of practice every bit as valid as the monastic path? Can suctioning the snot from a sick baby's nose have the simplicity and purity of a nun's prostrations? Can wiping out a diaper pail lead to 'the awakening of the Buddha and the ancestors'?

On one level, this question seems absurd. Nothing could be further from the regimented march of a formal retreat than the disheveled dance of motherhood. The books on my bedside table used to be about pursuing Awakening in the Himalayas. Now they're about preventing awakening in the middle of the night. There's a diaper changing table where my altar used to be; my zafus and zabutons have been requisitioned to cushion Skye's play area. Forget about chewing a single raisin for five minutes and admonitions to 'when you eat, just eat'—I'm on the phone with Skye on my hip, ordering baby-proof plates for the electrical outlets as I eat cold veggie potstickers with my fingers straight from the cardboard box and rub fresh spit-up into the floor with one socked foot. It's hard to find the moment even to tell myself that this is a spiritual path—I'm too busy looking for Skye's other mitten . . .

Could there be any better way to get my nose rubbed in the truth of impermanence than to love a child in a jagged, careless world? Napping with Skye in my king-size bed—his head on my breast, my nose pressed against the dark silk of his hair—I watch the heartbeat fluttering in the soft spot on his skull. Forget about freeways, and plutonium, and stealth bombers—I've been sternly warned that even a teddy bear could suffocate him in his crib. At night, when he's been silent a couple of hours, I creep into his room and stand in the dark, not moving for fear of creaking a floorboard, until I hear him sigh.

And even if everything goes absolutely perfectly, I know that this particular Skye—the one who warbles and passionately sucks on the bill of his rubber duck as he splashes with me in the tub—is going to dissolve like bubble bath. Yesterday he was a kicking bulge in my belly as I swam laps in the July sun; tomorrow he'll be a middle-aged man, weeping and scattering my ashes in a mountain lake. Watching Skye rub strained carrots into his eyelashes, my husband says, 'It's so beautiful that it hurts.'

I feel plugged into the world now, in a way that I never have been before. As I feed my child out of my own body, I see how I am fed by the body of the earth. I'm crocheted to a chain of mothers before me, and a chain of unborn children who will inherit a world that I can't even imagine. I want Skye's grandchildren to be able to swim in the Pacific, and hike the granite ridges of the Sierra, and gasp at the blue herons standing on one leg in Bolinas Lagoon.

Is this 'attachment'? Or connectedness?

I don't mean to be grandiose. I know these insights aren't the pristine diamond of samadhi. They're a sloppier, stickier kind of realization, covered in drool and Cheerio crumbs. But maybe this is the gift of mothering as practice—a kind of inclusiveness that embraces chaos and grit and imperfection. It's not based on control or keeping things tidy.

It makes room in its heart for a plastic dump truck in the middle of the living room floor, and rap music leaking under a bedroom door at midnight. It doesn't slip away in the middle of the night to search for enlightenment. It stays home with Rahula the Fetter, and finds it there.

As mothers, what can we make of that story of the Buddha leaving his family in the middle of the night?

I asked Fu Schroeder. 'Oh, but he wasn't the Buddha when he left his child. He was a young prince, in terrible pain,' she answered.

'If you're awake, you don't leave your child. Where would you go?'

bibliography

Abrams, Rebecca, 'She's Not My Little Baby Anymore', *Sydney's Child*, June 2001

American Association of Health Plans, Survey, Boston, 1996, 1997

Barber, Jim et al., 'Things Aren't so Bad at Home After All', *News, Events and Notices*, Flinders University, South Australia and La Trobe University, Victoria, 1998

Boorstein, Sylvia, *It's Easier Than You Think: The Buddhist Way to Happiness*, HarperCollins, San Francisco, 1995

Buddhadasa Bhikkhu, *Handbook for Mankind*, Dharma Study and Practice Group, Bangkok, 1988

Claxton, Guy, *The Heart of Buddhism: Practical Wisdom for an Agitated World*, Crucible, Northamptonshire, 1990

Cushman, Anne, 'Mothering as Meditation Practice', *Tricycle, The Buddhist Review*, Fall, 2001, p. 104

Dalai Lama, His Holiness the, *The Heart of the Buddha's Path*, Thorsons, London, 1999, p. 212

Dhammananda, Sri K., *How to Live Without Fear and Worry*, Buddhist Missionary Society, Kuala Lumpur, 1989

Dowrick, Stephanie, *Forgiveness and Other Acts of Love*, Penguin, Ringwood, Victoria, 1997

Dowrick, Stephanie, *The Universal Heart*, Viking Penguin Books, Ringwood, Victoria, 2000

Figes, Kate, *Life After Birth: What Even Your Friends Won't Tell You About Motherhood*, Viking, London, 1998, p. 84

Film Australia, *Myths of Childhood*, Sydney, 1998

Gawler, Dr Ian, *Peace of Mind*, Hill of Content, Melbourne, 1987

Geshe Kelsang Gyatso, *Understanding The Mind: An Explanation of the Nature and Functions of the Mind*, Tharpa, Cumbria, England, 1997

Geshe Kelsang Gyatso, *Transform Your Life: A Blissful Journey*, Tharpa, Cumbria, England, 2001

Gunaratana, Bhante Henepola, *Eight Mindful Steps to Happiness: Walking the Buddhas's Path*, Wisdom Publications, Boston, 2001, p. 78

Hagen, Steve, *Buddhism Plain and Simple: The Practice of Being Aware Right Now, Every Day*, Tuttle Publishing, New York, 1998

Henderson Julie, 'Tulku', in Lenore Friedman and Susan Moon (eds), *Being Bodies: Buddhist Women on the Paradox of Embodiment*, Shambhala, Boston, 1997, p. 220

Hope, Jane & Van Loon, Borin, *Buddha for Beginners*, Icon Books, Trumpington, Cambridge, 1994

Howley, Adrienne, *The Naked Buddha: A Simple Explanation of a 'New' Old Religion*, Bantam, Sydney, 1999, pp. 41, 172

Jandamit, Helen, *The Path to Peace Within: A Guide to Insight Mediation*, Gateway Books, Bath, 1997

Kabat-Zinn, Jon and Myla, *Everyday Blessings: The Inner Work of Mindful Parenting*, Hyperion, New York, 1997, p. 85

Kornfield, Jack, *A Path with Heart: A Guide Through the Perils and Promises of Spiritual Life*, Bantam Books, New York and Toronto, 1993, p. 291

Kornfield, Jack, *After the Ecstasy, the Laundry: How the Heart Grows Wise on the Spiritual Path*, Bantam Books, London, 2000

Landaw, Jonathan & Brooke, Janet, *Prince Siddhartha*, Wisdom, Boston, 1984

Larkin, Geri, *Stumbling Toward Enlightenment*, Celestial Arts, California, 1997

Mackenzie, Vicki, *Cave in the Snow: A Western Woman's Quest for Enlightenment*, Bloomsbury, London, 1998, p. 166

Mackenzie, Vicki, *Why Buddhism? Westerners in Search of Wisdom*, Allen & Unwin, Sydney, 2001, p. 283

Masters, Kamala, 'Just Washing Dishes', in Sharon Salzberg (ed), *Voices of Insight*, Shambhala, Boston, 1999, pp. 49–61

Rich, Adrienne, *Of Woman Born: Motherhood as Experience and Institution*, Virago, USA, 1977, p. 23

Salzberg, Sharon, *A Heart as Wide as the World: Stories on the Path of Lovingkindness*, Shambhala, Boston, 1997

Salzberg, Sharon, *Lovingkindness: The Revolutionary Art of Happiness*, Shambhala, Boston, 1997

Suzuki, Shunryu, *Zen Mind, Beginner's Mind*, Weatherhill, New York, 1970

Thich Nhat Hanh, *Teachings on Love*, Parallax Press, California, 1998, pp. 27, 66

Thurman, Robert, *Inner Revolution: Life, Liberty, and the Pursuit of Real Happiness*, Riverhead Books, New York, 1998, p. 81

Thynn, Thynn, *Living Meditation, Living Insight*, Sae Taw Win II Dharma Foundation, Sebastopol, California, 1998

Titmuss, Christopher, *Light on Enlightenment: Revolutionary Teachings on the Inner Life*, Shambhala, Boston, 1998

index